Books You Need
to do
Genealogy
in Ontario

an annotated bibliography

Ryan Taylor

ROUND
TOWER
BOOKS

FORT WAYNE   INDIANA   1996

Published by: ROUND TOWER BOOKS
Box 12407
Fort Wayne IN 46863-2407

© 1996 Ryan Taylor

Publisher's Cataloging in Publication Data

Taylor, Ryan.
     Books you need to do genealogy in Ontario ; an annotated bibliography.

List of publishers: p. 151-154.
ISBN: 0-9643925-1-8

    1. Ontario - Genealogy - Bibliography. I. T.

929.3 713 016

Printed in the United States of America
by Bookcrafters

For
Maureen Shepherd

with thanks for the encouragement,
the laughter, and the obits

Acknowledgements

First thanks are due to Steve Myers, my colleague and publisher, who encouraged this project from its conception.

Others answered questions regarding specific titles and made suggestions, for which I am grateful. The librarians of small institutions in northern Ontario were both patient and helpful in describing their resources. The telephone reference service of the Kitchener Public Library was, as always, first-rate.

Mary Bond and Sandra Burrows of the National Library made it possible for me to use the facilities in Ottawa with ease. Their ongoing assistance and interest demonstrate to me exactly what a national library is for.

Contents

General	4
Algoma	29
Brant	31
Bruce	34
Carleton	36
Cochrane	40
Dufferin	41
Dundas	41
Durham	42
Elgin	45
Essex	49
Frontenac	53
Glengarry	59
Grey	60
Haldimand	62
Haliburton	64
Halton	65
Hastings	67
Huron	69
Kenora	70
Kent	70
Lambton	75
Lanark	79
Leeds & Grenville	84
Lennox & Addington	88
Lincoln	92
Middlesex	94
Muskoka	97
Nipissing	97
Norfolk	98
Northumberland	103
Ontario county	105
Oxford	106
Parry Sound	110
Peel	111
Perth	112

Peterborough	114
Prescott	115
Prince Edward	116
Rainy River	118
Renfrew	118
Russell	120
Simcoe	121
Stormont	124
Sudbury	126
Thunder Bay	128
Timiskaming	128
Victoria	129
Waterloo	130
Welland	134
Wellington	138
Wentworth	141
York	145
List of Publishers	151

Introduction

One of the difficulties in genealogy lies in determining what useful printed materials are available, especially if the place involved is far away. This situation is aggravated by the subject headings for genealogical materials used in most libraries, which range from vague ("Genealogy" for everything, or "Registers of births, etc.") to purposely obfuscating ("Inscriptions" and "Sepulchral monuments" for cemetery markings). Researchers usually have to visit the ancestral area to find archival materials (although more of them are becoming available in microform), but printed books should be accessible for long distance research either through purchase or interlibrary loan.

The purpose of this bibliography is to provide a basic list of materials on Ontario genealogy which researchers can then use to access the information they need. As well as obvious genealogical resources, historical and background titles are given, to enable researchers to find materials which will assist them in compiling true family histories and not merely dry genealogies.

Many titles in the bibliography are recent and may still be purchased, so a list of publishers is also provided. The bibliographic information needed to apply for an interlibrary loan is also present. In addition, most titles are annotated to provide details which might not be obvious, and which will help determine if the book is what a researcher requires.

The titles listed are, with one or two exceptions, those which have been published for sale in printed form. Archival materials, even those which may have been bound in two or three copies for library use, are not included.

Generally, materials available only in microform are also not included, although there are references to older books which are not generally for sale now in paper format but may be purchased in microform. A huge number of these are available from the Canadian Institute for Historical Microreproduction (CIHM).

Bibliographies of certain classes of books have been published elsewhere. Local histories have been competently listed in Barbara Aitken's *Local histories of Ontario municipalities 1951-1977* and its supplement. These two books (which are still for sale from the Ontario Library Association) are reference tools which every Ontario genealogist should know. Titles listed in them have not been included here, with occasional exceptions. Local histories published since 1987 are included here, although I make no claim to be exhaustive, and Barbara Aitken plans a third volume which will add them to her list.

Directories can be found in Mary Bond's listing, with its extensive index. A few directory reprints are included in this bibliography, but researchers should always refer to Bond to determine the existence of directories they need. Many of those listed in Bond are available from CIHM.

Cemetery transcriptions would have doubled the size of this volume. Most are published by branches of the Ontario Genealogical Society (OGS) and can be found in its *Ontario Genealogical Society publications for sale 1995.* For each county, I have indicated who publishes cemeteries in that area; inquire from the publisher concerned.

Church histories and OGS branch surname directories are also not included. If I have encountered published versions of Tweedsmuir histories, they have been added, but most are only available in manuscript or on microfilm. Microtext versions are listed in Aitken. Nineteenth century books with recent reprint dates are given with the most recent bibliographic information, with the thought that these versions are the ones which will most readily be available on interlibrary loan. Original dates of publication are always given.

In the interest of saving space, multiple volumes of a similar nature have sometimes been conflated into one entry. For example, Susan Bergeron's series of census indexes for various Northumberland county townships and villages have been given one entry for each geographic entity.

In the nineteenth century there were a great many books published which described early life in Upper Canada/Canada West. Most genealogists will find these entertaining reading, broadening their understanding of their ancestors' pioneer existence and perhaps providing some colorful background quotations for a family history. A few of these, such as Guillet and Lamond, have been included. I urge anyone with an interest to search out titles which have been reprinted and are readily available in libraries, such as Susanna Moodie's *Roughing it in the Bush,* Catharine Parr Traill's *The Canadian Settler's Guide,* and *Twenty four years in Canada West* by their brother, Samuel Strickland.

For our American readers, the term 'strays' needs explaining. It has nothing to do with cattle. In a census index, a 'stray' is a person living in a house with a surname different from the head of the household. It may be a stepchild, servant, in-law or visitor.

A Geographical Note

If your geographical knowledge of an ancestor's home area is incomplete, I urge you to study it before proceeding in your research. For people so wedded to the landscape as the pioneers, geography had a huge influence. Also, factors such as duplicated geographical names (common in Ontario) will confuse you if you are unprepared. For example, the town of Perth, in eastern Ontario, has no connection with the county of Perth, in the west.

The county names used in this book are pre-1972.

One advantage of a listing of this kind is to enable people to explore areas which are near our ancestors' homes but across an artificial political boundary. Newspapers do not only contain references to people from their own county; church records may encompass a broad area. For instance, the Beachville register in Oxford county listed here is said to include materials from other counties. The Tillsonburg funeral home records were published by Elgin County branch OGS because they included so many Elgin county people, although Tillsonburg is well inside Oxford county. I hope that readers will take advantage of this single listing to consider which materials from neighboring counties may well include their relations' names.

Use a map in conjunction with the list, checking which large towns might have attracted your ancestors. Kemptville was the place to shop for many in southern Carleton county, although it was across a border. Transportation routes, such as the Rideau Canal, would also have affected where people went for baptizing, marrying or burying.

Most of the books listed here can be found at the Allen County Public Library, Fort Wayne, Indiana.

No list of this kind can be complete in any sense. Suggestions for a future edition or supplement would be welcomed; write to me at the Allen County Public Library, Box 2270, Fort Wayne IN USA 46801-2270.

Fort Wayne   R.T.
January 1996

General

Barbara B. Aitken. *Local histories of Ontario municipalities, 1951-1977: a bibliography.* Toronto: Ontario Library Association, 1978. 120pp. ISBN: 0-88969-012-X.

Listed alphabetically by subject. This was followed by a supplement *Local histories of Ontario municipalities, 1977-1987: a bibliography* (1989; ISBN: 0-88969-030-8). These cover the most important era of local history publication in Ontario, particularly circa 1967, when Canada's centennial provoked a great deal of writing. SEE Introduction for further discussion.

American library directory. New Providence, N.J.: R.R.Bowker. Annual, 2 v. each year. ISSN: 0065-910X.

Despite its title, Canada is included at the end of volume 2. This lists all libraries by place, with details of address, telephone, special collections and budgets. It is a must-know for genealogists, who can use it to determine the correct library to consult in a certain area, and its proper address. It can be found in all libraries.

W. Bruce Antliff. *Loyalist settlements, 1783-1789: new evidence of Canadian Loyalist claims.* Toronto: Archives of Ontario/Ministry of Citizenship and Culture, 1985. 423pp. ISBN: 0-7743-9890-6 (hardcover ed.) Indexed.

An attempt to coordinate Loyalist evidence in its various archives, including newly-published material and an index. Very important. Published in conjunction with a microfiche edition of the Ontario Bureau of Archives' report for 1904 (q.v.) and a portfolio of maps and documents.

Frederick H. Armstrong. *Handbook of Upper Canadian chronology and territorial legislation.* London: Lawson Memorial Library, University of Western Ontario, 1967. 233pp.

"...tables of officials, parliaments and legislation..." including both elected and appointed office-holders, up to the 1840s.

Eunice Ruiter Baker. *Searching for your ancestors in Canada.* Ottawa: Heritage House, 1975. 80pp.

Much outdated early introduction to the subject.

Angus Baxter. *In search of your Canadian roots.* Toronto: Macmillan, 1989. xviii,350pp. Bibliography. Index..

Updated successor to his *In search of your roots* (1978) which also had a Canadian theme. The Ontario chapter provides a useful quick overview, very much emphasizing the Archives of Ontario. Its contents may be misleading, because a great deal more is available than can be listed in a few pages, so serious genealogists requiring detailed information should refer instead to Merriman (q.v.).

Carol Bennett. *Peter Robinson's settlers.* Renfrew: Juniper Books, 1987. 195pp., illus. ISBN: 0-919137-16-4. Index.

Robinson sponsored a large Irish emigration to Bathurst and Newcastle districts in the 1820s, although the ones in Peterborough are best known. Bennett says, "I wanted to list all the families, with their place of origin in Ireland and their location here." Alphabetical.

Carol Bennett & D.W. McCuaig. *Valley Irish.* Renfrew: Juniper Books, 1983. 114pp., illus. ISBN: 0-919137-07-5. Index.

Brief accounts, ranging across Ireland as well as through the Ottawa valley, including some family histories.

Mary E. Bond. *Canadian directories, 1790-1987: a bibliography and place-name index.* Ottawa: National Library of Canada, 1989. 3v. ISBN: 0-660-54786-4 (set) Bibliography.

Successor to Ryder. It is a listing of the directories in the National Library and National Archives library (since transferred to the National Library). It includes about 1200 entries, followed by a place-name index for the many smaller localities included, and comprising 21,500 entries. Many of the pre-1900 directories are available for sale on microfiche from CIHM. The introduction is recommended reading.

Arthur Bousfield & Garry Toffoli. *Loyalist vignettes and sketches.* Toronto: Governor Simcoe Branch, UEL Association of Canada, 1984. 183pp., illus.

Brief essays on individual loyalists.

Elizabeth Briggs. *Access to ancestry: a genealogical resources manual for Canadians tracing their heritage.* Winnipeg, MB: Westgarth, 1995. 166pp., charts. ISBN: 0-9697453-1-1. Indexed.

Despite the title, this is essentially a handbook for Manitoba genealogy. The other provinces receive a few pages each.

W.E. Britnell and Elizabeth Hancocks. *County marriage registers of Ontario, Canada, 1858-1869.* Agincourt: Generation Press, 1979- (in progress). ISBN: 0-920830-00-5 (set)

From 1858 to 30 June 1869, Ontario had a semi-formal method of marriage registration, recorded in ledgers in Toronto. These index the ledgers. The early volumes are indexes only and require consultation with the originals (available on microfilm); later volumes give the complete information excepting witnesses, clergy's name and church. Confirmation with the originals is recommended. Most volumes cover one county.

Paul J. Bunnell. *The new Loyalist index.* Bowie, MD : Heritage Books, 1989. 1 v. (unpaged). ISBN: 1-55613-234-4. Indexed.

Computerized index with brief references; heavy emphasis on Maritime provinces with some Ontario material.

Paul J. Bunnell. *Research guide to Loyalist ancestors: a directory to archives, manuscripts and published sources.* Bowie, MD : Heritage Books, 1990. 146pp. Bibliographical references.

Brief sections on all Canadian provinces and territories, some American states, England and other colonies.

Sandra Burrows & Franceen Gaudet. *Checklist of indexes to Canadian newspapers.* Ottawa: National Library of Canada, 1987. 148pp. ISBN: 0-660-53735-4. Indexed.

"The first comprehensive listing of indexes to Canadian newspapers...the result of a survey sent to 4000 institutions across Canada." (Preface) Organized by institution, with indexes of journal names and places. An updated listing of those at the NLC is in Ketchum (q.v.)

Mary Byers & Margaret McBurney. *The Governor's Road: early buildings and families from Mississauga to London.* Toronto: University of Toronto Press, 1982. 319pp., illus. ISBN: 0-8020-2482-1. Index.

Houses, families and settlements along the first highway west from Lake Ontario.

Wendy Cameron & Mary McDougall Maude. *The Petworth emigration scheme: a preliminary list of emigrants from Sussex and neighbouring counties in England to Upper Canada, 1832-1837.* Toronto: Wordforce, 1990. 25pp.

    Part of an ongoing project to document settlers sponsored by Lord Egremont (of Petworth). The emigrants settled in pockets in Wentworth, Middlesex and elsewhere. Further details of the project appear annually in *Families* (q.v.). A full list and documentation is slated to appear in 1996.

Canadian gazetteer SEE *Smith's Canadian Gazetteer*

William Canniff. *The settlement of Upper Canada.* Belleville: Mika, 1971. 671,27pp. Index.

    Originally published in Toronto in 1869. This edition includes an index of personal names.

Floreen Ellen Carter. *Place names of Ontario.* London: Phelps, 1984. 2v. ISBN: 0920298397 (set). Bibliographic references.

    Very useful for locating villages, towns and other settlements by their former names. Disused names listed with reference to the earliest. Originally in print briefly, so difficult to find in paper format. Reissued on microfiche by Information Graphics, currently available.

The centennial of the settlement of Upper Canada... SEE *The old United Empire Loyalists list.*

Edward Marion Chadwick. *Ontarian families: genealogies of United Empire Loyalist and other pioneer families of Upper Canada.* Toronto: Smith, Rolph, 1894-98. 2 v.

    112 socially prominent families. Reprinted several times in recent years, sometimes in a one-volume edition; also available on microform from UMI.

Edward Marion Chadwick. *Ontarian genealogist and family historian.* Toronto: Rolph, Smith, 1898-1901. 12 numbers.

    Chadwick's intention was to publish Loyalist or "old pioneer" genealogies, updating *Ontarian families* (above). The format used is that of the peerage. Available on microfiche from CIHM (1989).

Christian Messenger, births, deaths, marriages. Hamilton: Hamilton branch OGS, 1975?- . (in progress)

Title varies; that given is for most recent volumes. Extracts, with full text given, from a Baptist newspaper based in southwestern Ontario but covering the whole province. Volumes 1-13 cover 1854 to 1877. The originals are at McMaster University.

The Civil Service List. Ottawa: Queen's Printer. (many volumes)

The title of this publication varies, but this is the most common. It is also known as *Return shewing the names, origin, creed, position and pay of all the employés of the Dominion Government* (1872 edition), which sums up what you find. Best of all it gives the date of employment. Some of the early eds. (such as *The Blue Book...of the Province of Canada 1867)* were produced by commercial publishers. As well as Ottawa workers, it includes all the customs officials in all provinces, railway, inland revenue and fisheries people (of whom there are a great many). Although it is rare in other libraries, the National Library has a considerable run.

Norman K. Crowder. ***British army pensioners abroad, 1772-1899.*** Baltimore: Genealogical Publishing, 1995. xviii,351pp. Bibliography. Index.

Norman K. Crowder. ***Early Ontario settlers: a source book***. Baltimore: Genealogical Publishing, 1993. xx,239pp., maps. ISBN: 0-8063-1375-7. Bibliographical references and index.

Virginia Easley DeMarce. ***The settlement of former German auxiliary troops in Canada after the American revolution.*** Sparta, Wisc.: Joy Reisinger, 1984. 350pp. ISBN: 916849-02-3. Indexed.

Useful dictionary of soldiers with references to archival sources for each. Cover title: *German military settlers in Canada after the American revolution.*

Dictionary of Canadian biography. Toronto: University of Toronto Press, 1966-   (in progress) ISBN: 0-8020-3142-0 (v.1). Bibliographical references.

Volumes are organized by date of death of the individual; twelve volumes published currently covering 1000-1900. There is an overall *Index* for the 12 volumes.

Bryan Lee Dilts. *1848 and 1850 Canada West (Ontario) census index; an every name index.* Salt Lake City, Utah: Index Publishing, 1984. 121pp. ISBN 0-914311-24-7.

Only fragments of these censuses survive, but this covers the whole province.

Directory of Canadian archives. Ottawa: Canadian Council of Archives, 1990. xiii,130pp. Text in English and French.

The alphabetizing of this directory is odd, but it is due to be replaced by a new edition in 1996.

Arthur Garratt Dorland. *The Quakers in Canada: a history.* Toronto: Ryerson Press, 1968. xi,360pp., illus. Bibliography. Indexed.

Histories of individual meetings as well as an overview. Many names.

Althea Douglas & J. Creighton Douglas. *Canadian railway records: a guide for genealogists.* Toronto: Ontario Genealogical Society, 1994. 64pp. ISBN: 1-55116-932-0.

Brief history of railways in Canada with pointers for those who have relations employed by them.

Dundas Mission register, 1840-1853. Delhi: Norfolk County branch OGS, n.d. 126pp. Index.

The Roman Catholic mission at Dundas had far-reaching responsibilities in Wentworth, Oxford, Brant, Haldimand and Norfolk. Baptisms, marriages and burials are included, full text and indexes.

B. Mabel Dunham. *Grand River.* Toronto: McClelland and Stewart, 1945. 299pp., maps.

Readable introduction to the early history of this river valley which runs through Waterloo, Wellington, Brant and Haldimand counties.

Early Methodist records. s.l.: Bay of Quinte branch, U.E.L. Association, n.d. 17pp. Index.

Circuit riders' records from Smith Creek, Bay of Quinte and Napanee circuits, 1805-1853. Includes areas in later Durham, Northumberland, Hastings, Prince Edward, Lennox & Addington and Frontenac counties.

Noel Montgomery Elliot. *The Central Canadians 1600-1900: an alphabetized directory of the people, places and vital dates.* Toronto: Genealogical Research Library, 1995. 3 v. ISBN: 0-919941-17-6 (set).

Half a million entries for individuals in Ontario and Manitoba resources. This is an expanded and greatly improved version of *People of Ontario 1600-1900*. Includes place-name index. Provides name, time period and place. Useful for finding lost people.

Noel Montgomery Elliot. *People of Ontario 1600-1900: alphabetized directory of the people, places and vital dates.* Toronto: Genealogical Research Library, 1984. 4 v. ISBN: 0-919941-00-1 (set)

Superseded by his *The Central Canadians*, above.

Bruce S. Elliott. *Index to the 1871 census of Ontario.* Toronto: Ontario Genealogical Society. 30v. ISBN: 0-920036-24-4 (Simcoe)

Heads of families and strays index covering the whole province. One volume per county, with some counties sharing a volume.

Bruce S. Elliott, Dan Walker, Fawne Stratford-Devai. *Men of Upper Canada: militia nominal rolls, 1828-1829.* Toronto: Ontario Genealogical Society, 1995. 356pp. ISBN: 0-7779-0188-9. Index.

"...the returns constitute the closest thing to a province-wide census that survives for a genealogically difficult period..."

Families. Toronto: OGS, 1971- . Quarterly journal. ISSN: 0030-2945.

Numbered from v. 10 (1971); volumes 1-9 bear title Ontario Genealogical Society *Bulletin.* Genealogical documents, essays, guides, plus reviews and queries. More transient news is published in *Newsleaf* (also quarterly and published at the same time). London branch has prepared an *Index* to names in the queries section; an overall *Index* is in preparation. Also indexed in the Canadian Periodical Index and PERSI (q.v.). A source of vital information which may not appear elsewhere.

R.C. Fetherstonhaugh. *McGill University at war, 1914-18, 1939-1945.* Montreal: McGill University, 1947. 437pp., illus. Indexed.

Includes lists of student-soldiers with details of both service and academic standing. Although this university is in Quebec, many people from Ontario go there. Similar books may be found for other colleges.

E.Keith Fitzgerald. *Ontario people: 1796-1803.* Baltimore: Genealogical Publishing, 1993. xi,250pp., maps. ISBN: 0-8063-1366-8. Index.

Nick G. Forte & Gabriele Scardellato. *A guide to the collections of the Multicultural History Society of Ontario.* Toronto: Multicultural History Society of Ontario, 1992. xx,695pp. ISBN: 0-919045-58-8. Index.

    Materials are listed by ethnic group. The collections are extensive and easily accessed by researchers.

Patricia C. Gallinger & Josephine Boos. *Ministerial record of Reverend Robert Barnes Beynon, July 1896-December 1940, nominal index.* Barrie: Shenrone Enterprises, 1991. 117pp., maps.

    Beynon lived in Grey, Simcoe, York and Peel counties; all are represented. He was a Methodist minister and the records include baptisms, marriages and burials.

Herbert Fairbairn Gardiner. *Nothing but names: an inquiry into the origin of the names of the counties and townships of Ontario.* Toronto: Morang, 1899. 561pp. Index.

    Less scientific than Carter (q.v.) but an amusing resource.

Franceen Gaudet: SEE Sandra Burrows; Sheila Ketchum.

Gazetteer of Canada: Ontario. Ottawa: Published for the Canadian Permanent Committee on Geographic Names, by Surveys and Mapping Branch, Department of Energy, Mines and Resources, 1977. 2d ed. xxxiii,823pp., map.

    Locations only, no explanations. Also available on microfiche. Updated by supplements.

June Gibson. *Surrogate court index of Ontario, Canada, 1859-1900.* Agincourt: Generation Press, 1988- . (in progress). ISBN: 0-920830-34-X (v.1).

    Index to wills and probate records now held at the Archives of Ontario. Gives name, place of residence, year and file number. With this information genealogists can obtain copies of the files from the Archives. Most volumes cover one county.

J. Brian Gilchrist. *Inventory of Ontario newspapers 1793-1986.* Toronto: Micromedia, 1987. vi,202,74pp. ISBN: 0-88892-596-4. Index.

    The most complete list of newspapers, with publication history and current locations. Beware: it uses the post-1972 official town names, which is confusing for genealogists.

Peter Gillis, David Hume, Robert Armstrong. *Records relating to Indian Affairs (RG 10).* Ottawa: Public Archives of Canada, 1975. 50pp.

    The Archives' Public Records division, General Inventory Series, no. 1. For those with native ancestry, this is a handy reference tool.

A guide to Ontario land registry records. Toronto: Ontario Genealogical Society, 1994. 42pp., 16 plates. ISBN: 0-7779-0184-6. Bibliography.

    Introductory guidebook prepared for the Archives of Ontario with genealogists in mind. Basic for all researchers.

Guide to the holdings of the ecclesiastical province of Ontario. Agincourt: Generation Press, 1990. 367pp. Index.

    This is a list of materials in the Anglican diocesan and synodical archives, so it is a guide to what parish records are *not* deposited as well as those that are. Note that this is for the ecclesiastical province, which is slightly different from the geographical province (and there is also a separate diocese with the same name). Kenora is in the diocese of Keewatin, whose archives are in Winnipeg.

Edwin C. Guillet. *Early Life in Upper Canada.* Toronto: Ontario Publishing, 1933. xliii,782pp., illus.

    For those who want to know how their ancestors lived in Ontario, this is the best work. It has been reprinted in smaller versions with individual topics (*Pioneer inns and taverns, Pioneer arts and crafts, Pioneer settlements*) in the 1950s and 1960s; copies of these later editions are common in second-hand shops. Highly recommended background reading.

Elizabeth Hancocks. *Townships and county seats of Ontario.* Toronto: Ontario Genealogical Society, n.d. 9 leaves, maps.

    A listing of townships in the old (pre-1972) counties, with maps showing each.

Elizabeth Hancocks   SEE ALSO W. E. Britnell.

Andrew Haydon. *Pioneer sketches in the district of Bathurst.* Toronto: Ryerson Press, 1925. 291pp., illus. Index.
   Although described as "volume 1" on the title page, no more were published. Written in a more orotund 19th century style, but including many names.

Robert J. Hayward. *Fire insurance plans in the National Map Collection.* Ottawa: Public Archives of Canada, 1977. 171pp.
   Fire insurance maps zero in on the exact buildings on a property, enabling you to reconstruct the size and shape of your ancestor's house and its outbuildings.

Carolyn A. Heald. *The Irish Palatines in Ontario: religion, ethnicity and rural migration.* Gananoque: Langdale Press, 1994. 195pp., illus. ISBN: 1-895158-06-0. Bibliographical references. Index.
   Despite its academic title, this book offers a very accessible account of the origins of the Irish Palatines from a Canadian perspective.

Peter Hessel. *Destination: Ottawa Valley.* Ottawa: Runge Press, n.d. 161pp. ISBN: 0-9691976-0-8. Bibliography. Index.
   A description of German settlers in the Ottawa valley.

Thomas A. Hillman. *Catalogue of census returns on microfilm, 1666-1891.* Ottawa: Public Archives of Canada, 1987. 289pp. ISBN: 0-660-53711-7.
   Listing of places with census subdivisions for each year, and the official NAC film numbers. A basic publication for locating places on the microfilm. The 1901 census has a separate publication (below). The 1963 edition (*Check-list of Ontario census returns, 1842-1871*), still available in some libraries, includes microfilm numbers which no longer exist and should not be used.

Thomas A. Hillman. *Catalogue of census returns on microfilm, 1901.* Ottawa: National Archives of Canada, 1993. 196pp. ISBN: 0-660-57410-1.
   See above.

Frances Hoffman & Ryan Taylor. *Much to be done: private life in Ontario from Victorian diaries.* Toronto: Natural Heritage/Natural History, 1996. 253pp., illus.

    A discussion of life in Ontario using diary extracts as examples; may be used as a source of background material for family histories. Includes, for the first time anywhere, a bibliography of existing women's diaries in public archival collections.

Ruth Holt & Margaret Williams. *Genealogical extraction and index of the Canada Company remittance books, 1843-1847.* Weston: R.Holt, 1990. 3 v.

    The Canada Company's land was in western Ontario; the introduction to these volumes is a handy guide to its work. In many cases, places of origin in Britain and Ireland are mentioned.

Louise I. Hope. *Index to Niagara conference, Methodist Episcopal church, baptismal register, 1849-1886.* Toronto: Ontario Genealogical Society, 1994. 2 v. ISBN: 0-7779-0186-2 (v.1)

    Similar to the records for the Wesleyan Methodists, but for only part of the province, covering a good deal of Ontario west of Toronto. Parents' names and place-names included.

Herbert Karl Kalbfleisch. *The history of the pioneer German language press of Ontario, 1835-1918.* Toronto: University of Toronto Press, 1968. 133pp. Index.

    Researchers with German ancestry should consult this list of newspapers to determine which ones may contain family information. The newspapers travelled great distances to outlying German settlements.

Sheila Ketchum. *Checklist of indexes to Canadian newspapers held by the National Library of Canada.* Ottawa: National Library of Canada, 1992 (draft only). 26 leaves.

    Original list by Franceen Gaudet was dated 1987; this update has a limited circulation. Useful for those looking for indexes at the National Library; ask for it in the reading room there. This may be regarded as an adjunct to Burrows (q.v.).

Gilles Langelier. *National map collection.* Ottawa: Public Archives of Canada, 1985. 71pp.
    Part of the NAC's General Guide Series 1983. DSS cat. no. SA41-4/1-8. A description of the collection, its services and publications. For persons searching for specialized maps in Ontario, this is one place to start. The list of publications is especially valuable for genealogical research.

Robert Lamond. *A narrative of the rise & progress of emigration from the counties of Lanark & Renfrew, to the new settlements in Upper Canada....* Ottawa: Canadian Heritage Publications, 1978. 112pp. ISBN: 0-920648-01-0. Index.
    Originally published in Glasgow, 1831. No names, but provides detailed instructions about how to emigrate, including what to take. Useful to obtain a picture of what our ancestors brought with them. American researchers may find it easier to locate another edition prepared by Carey McWilliams, published by the Sutro branch, California state library in 1940 as their Occasional papers, reprint series no. 12. For English emigrants, read William Catermole's *Emigration: the advantages of emigration to Canada* (1831; republished by Coles 1970).

Wilfred R. Lauber. *An index of land claim certificates of Upper Canada militiamen who served in the war of 1812-1814.* Toronto: Ontario Genealogical Society, 1995. 136pp.
    Index only of original materials in the National Archives of Canada. There may be more than one document for each individual.

Edwin A. Livingston. *Johnstown district marriages, 1801-1851.* Prescott: Livingston, 1987. 108pp. ISBN: 0-920992-27-7. Index.
    Extracted from the original records, on microfilm at the NAC and Archives of Ontario. Full information is given.

Mildred R. Livingston. *Upper Canada sons and daughters of United Empire Loyalists.* Prescott: Livingston, 1981. 139pp. ISBN: 0-920992-08-0. Index.
    Extractions from Orders in Council: name, residence, status, name of parent, date. A second volume (announced) has not yet been published.

Loyalist families of the Grand River branch, United Empire Loyalists' Association of Canada. Toronto: Pro Familia, 1991. 667pp., illus. Index.

Genealogies showing descent from the Loyalist to the current UEL member.

Loyalist Lineages of Canada, 1783-1983. Agincourt: Generation Press; Toronto: Toronto Branch, United Empire Loyalists' Association of Canada, 1984-1991. 3 v. ISBN: 0-920830-24-2 (v.1); 0-9695178-0-7 (v.2 set). Indexed.

Volume one was published as an Ontario bicentennial project; the second volume (in two parts) commemorates the establishment of Upper Canada in 1791. All three volumes consist of members' genealogies, tracing the line from the Loyalist ancestor to contemporary persons.

Loyalist provisioning lists 1786. St. Catharines: Niagara Peninsula Branch OGS, n.d. 5pp. ISBN: 1-55034-322-X.

Descriptions of families drawing provisions at Niagara and Fort Erie soon after their emigration from the south.

C. Glenn Lucas. *The Evolution of various Christian denominations in Ontario.* Goderich: Huron County branch OGS, 1983. unpaged, maps. Bibliography.

The religious history of the province, area by area; good background for the researcher. The maps are useful, but the United Church Archives' one-page chart of the development of the United Church of Canada is not, alas, included.

A. David McFall and Jean McFall. *Land records in Ontario registry offices.* Toronto: Ontario Genealogical Society, 1984. 2d ed. 16pp. ISBN: 0-920036-12-0.

Basic material for researchers in Ontario. Brief and thorough introduction to the subject and addresses of the registry offices. Includes a history of the land copybooks by Shirley Spragge. An updated list of the addresses following reforms in the Ontario government can be found in *Families* v. 31, no. 4 (November 1992). A complete list of the copybooks and their locations is in *Families* v. 28, no. 3 (August 1989).

Donald A. McKenzie. *Death notices from the Canada Christian advocate, 1858-1872.* Lambertville, NJ: Hunterdon House, 1992. viii,384pp. Indexed.
See below.

Donald A. McKenzie. *Death notices from the Christian guardian, 1836-1850.* Lambertville, NJ: Hunterdon House, 1982. 375pp. Indexed.
Death notices from a religious newspaper which covered the whole province. The entries following this one give the names of other volumes in the series. Religious newspapers of the time often carried more of this kind of news than local papers, and were widely read. McKenzie's extensive work in the Methodist papers has made him an authority.

Donald A. McKenzie. *Death notices from the Christian guardian, 1851-1860.* Lambertville, NJ: Hunterdon House, 1984. vi,365pp. Indexed.
See above.

Donald A. McKenzie. *More notices from Methodist papers, 1830-1857.* Lambertville, NJ: Hunterdon House, 1986. xii,424pp. Indexed.
See above.

Donald. A. McKenzie. *More notices from Ontario's Methodist papers, 1858-1872.* s.l.: D. McKenzie, 1993. xii,321pp. Indexed.
See above.

Donald A. McKenzie. *Obituaries from Ontario's Christian guardian, 1861-1870.* Lambertville, NJ: Hunterdon House, 1988. ix,405pp. Indexed.
See above.

Donald A. McKenzie. *Upper Canada naturalization records, 1828-1850.* Toronto: OGS, 1991. 88pp.
An index to all pre-1850 records. Records of the 1840s are particularly useful, giving date of arrival in Canada and occasional exact birthplace.

Heather Maddick. *County maps: land ownership maps of Canada in the 19th century.* Ottawa: National Map Collection, Public Archives of Canada, 1976. 94pp., maps. ISBN: 0-662-00108-7. Indexed.

A listing of maps in the NAC which may aid genealogists. The introductory essay is brief and helpful: worth reading. SEE ALSO: May

Betty May. *County atlases of Canada: a descriptive catalogue.* Ottawa: National Map Collection, Public Archives of Canada, 1970. xii,192pp., maps.

Similar to Maddick above but for atlases. Includes lists of names of those whose portraits appear in 19th century atlases.

Brenda Dougall Merriman. *Genealogy in Ontario: searching the records.* Toronto: Ontario Genealogical Society, 1988. 2d ed. xiv,166pp., illus. ISBN: 1-55034-311-4. Indexed, extensive bibliography.

First ed. 1984. A revision is due in 1996. This is the basic handbook for Ontario research, with a useful bare-facts approach, addresses (some outdated by 1996), and advice. It tends to be Toronto-centred, with an emphasis on material available at the Archives of Ontario. A must for any Ontario genealogist.

Nick and Helma Mika. *Community spotlight: Leeds, Frontenac, Lennnox and Addington, and Prince Edward counties.* Belleville: Mika, 1974. 301pp., illus. ISBN: 0-919302-82-3.

Brief histories of 52 small places in these counties, some as large as Gananoque, or as small as Odessa.

Nick and Helma Mika. *Place names in Ontario: their name origins and history.* Belleville: Mika, 1977. 3 v., maps. ISBN: 0-919303-14-5 (v.1). Bibliographical references and index.

Localities and brief descriptions of founding. For some larger places, mini-essays giving historical highlights. Interesting, but not as complete as Carter (q.v.), which is a better reference tool.

Nick and Helma Mika. *United Empire Loyalists, pioneers of Upper Canada.* Belleville: Mika, 1976. 256pp., illus. ISBN: 0-919303-09-9. Index.

A general introduction, but with fewer names than might be hoped.

J.R. Ernest Miller & Robert E. Sargeant. *Early settlers to Bathurst district arriving prior to 1822.* Kingston: Kingston branch OGS, 1988. 52pp. ISBN: 1-55034-036-0.

The sources listed are: "Microfilm ISBN 1-55034-025-5; Col. Marshall's 1834 report; 1842 census of area, baptismal records of Rev. William Bell," but none are cited with individual entries, which are in a brief computer format. Regarding the microfilm, the authors state, "it was difficult to read and all information contained was not extracted."

J.R. Ernest Miller. *Scottish settlers to Bathurst area for Bathurst district; includes Lanark, Leeds, Carleton, Frontenac and Renfrew settlers, extracted from Dictionary of Scottish Settlers and other sources.* Kingston: Kingston branch OGS, 1987. 24pp. ISBN: 1-55034-037-9.

Plus two supplements (18 & 4 pp.) Abbreviated computer format and no sources given, but may provide a research clue.

R.Robert Mutrie. *Ontario marriages, 1869.* Ridgeway: Log Cabin Publishing, 1995.

First of a series (1870, 1871 and 1872 are to follow). The computerized index to the Ontario Vital Records beginning in 1869 uses the old handwritten index for these years. This is an attempt to create a new index. Full details of the marriages are given. Indexed by name of bride and groom.

Gerald J. Neville. *The Lanark Society settlers: ships' lists of the Glasgow Emigration Society, 1821.* Ottawa: British Isles Family History Society of Greater Ottawa, 1995. 60pp. ISBN: 1-896521-00-2. Index.

Their Publication no. 1. Lists by sponsoring group, with full details of ages and payments.

Niagara conference Methodist missionary report, 1885-86. Brantford: Brant County branch OGS, 1984. 15pp.

Photocopy of the original report, which lists churches and amounts paid by parishioners. Counties covered: Lincoln, Welland, Norfolk, Oxford, Wentworth, Brant, Halton. Useful as a locating tool, as it falls halfway between censuses.

N.L. Nicholson. *The maps of Canada; a guide to official Canadian maps, charts, atlases and gazetteers.* Folkstone, England: Wm. Dawson & Sons, 1981. 251pp. Bibliographical references. Index.

Not a catalog, but a description, which may lead to maps you did not know existed. For the experienced researcher.

The Old United Empire Loyalists list. Baltimore: Genealogical Publishing, 1984. vi,334pp. ISBN: 0-8063-0331-X.

Originally published 1885 as *The centennial of the settlement of Upper Canada by the United Empire Loyalists, 1784-1884...* and again by Genealogical Publishing in 1969. This list cannot be viewed as entirely accurate any longer, but is a useful starting point for many researchers.

Ontario Bureau of Archives. *Report.* Toronto: L.K. Cameron, Queen's Printer, 1904-1920. 15 v., illus. Annual.

These reports contain a great deal of original documentary material and are worth spending some time with. The most important is 1904 (published 1905), which includes the Loyalist material. It has been reprinted in both paper and microfiche several times, most notably in fiche as part of the Archives of Ontario's bicentenary publication (see Antliff, above) and reproduced in paper by Genealogical Publishing, 1994.

Ontario Genealogical Society. *Directory of surnames.*

Published from time to time by the Society. The format varies, but it is a listing of names and OGS members who are researching them. Members may submit entries. There are now a number of volumes, each of which is different.

Ontario Genealogical Society. *Seminar annual.*

The fourth issue each year of *Families* (q.v.) once contained printed versions of selected speeches given at the annual OGS Seminar. When this became problematic, they were, for a year or two, issued separately. Now, following the American example, each Seminar has a syllabus with either complete versions or notes and references for the speeches. All of these volumes can be found readily in libraries and may be worth discovering. The quality of syllabus materials varies.

Ontario Genealogical Society branch newsletters.

Each OGS branch has a newsletter, some of which now go back 25 years and more. Although they vary in quality (and each varies from editor to editor), most will provide information on genealogical resources which is available nowhere else. Many libraries maintain long runs, especially of their local branch, and all branch newsletters are indexed in *PERSI* (q.v.).

Ontario Genealogical Society publications for sale 1995. Toronto: OGS, 1995. 150pp. ISBN: 0-7779-0187-0.
   A listing of all current publications for OGS and its branches. Since most of these are cemeteries, it is a handy reference tool as well. First published 1993.

Ontario Historical Society. *Papers and records.* Toronto: Wm. Briggs, 1899-
   Assorted historical documents, essays and other resources, frequently neglected by genealogists. It is widely available in libraries, and there is a published *Index.*

The Ontario register. Lambertville, NJ: Hunterdon House, 1968-1989. 8v.
   This unusual periodical provided access to a variety of Ontario documents before they became more generally available through indexes or microfilm. The volumes appeared irregularly and it was suspended for several years in the 1980s before a final volume appeared. It can be found widely in libraries and is worth consulting, especially if you have research before 1850.

Charles Pinch. *Anglicanism in Ancaster from 1790 to 1830.* Ancaster: Ancaster Township Historical Society, n.d. various pagings. ISBN: 0-9692390-1-7. Bibliographical references.
   Despite its title, it covers a broad section of Niagara and central western Ontario. Republishes baptisms, weddings and burials at Niagara, 1792-ca.1830, previously published by the Ontario Historical Society, baptisms & marriages from the London and Gore districts, 1816-1827 and Ancaster parish registers 1830-1838, with a history of the parish.

PERiodical Source Index (PERSI). Fort Wayne, Ind. : Allen County Public Library Foundation, 1986-   . (in progress)
   The only substantive genealogical periodicals index, covering materials internationally. About 4500 journals are indexed, including *Families* (the OGS quarterly) and all OGS branch newsletters. As well as current issues, there are retrospective volumes going back to the 1840s. In Ontario, *PERSI* is available at public libraries in North York, Toronto, Ottawa, London, Windsor and St. Catharines.

Julia Pine. *Ontario's amazing museums: a guide to Ontario's most interesting and unusual museums, archives, education centres and collections.* Toronto: E C W Press, c1994. viii,290pp. ISBN: 1-55022-208-2. Indexed.

Although many of the museums will not be helpful to genealogists, some have archives of note. Researchers should be aware of specialized collections such as the National Ballet of Canada Archives if you have a dancer in the family. Also a useful guide for those planning genealogical trips and who have spouses/children to amuse.

Dora Pineau. *The marriage register of the Western district, 1796-1856.* Windsor: Essex County branch OGS, 1993. 89pp.

Extracted from the original, with full details including witnesses.

Pioneer life on the Bay of Quinte, including geneaologies [sic] of old families and biographical sketches of representative citizens. Belleville: Mika, 1972. 1005pp. ISBN: 0-919302-28-9.

Originally published circa 1905 in Toronto. From the new introduction: "...comprised of histories and genealogies of about 325 families... The region of settlement embraced by this volume is wider than its title might suggest, extending roughly from Kingston to Trenton, and covering the counties of Frontenac, Lennox and Addington, Hastings and Prince Edward." Some genealogies extend back to the beginning of American settlement.

Polyphony: bulletin of the Multicultural History Society of Ontario. Toronto: The Society, 1978- . ISSN: 0704-7002.

This biannual publication's many special issues on specific ethnic groups in the province (*Poles in Ontario*) or specific cities (*Toronto's People; Sudbury's People*) could be useful for researchers. Some contain reminiscences of individuals, and all have pictures and bibliographical references.

J.F. Pringle. *Lunenburgh or the old Eastern district, its settlement and early progress, with personal recollections of the town of Cornwall from 1824 to which are added a history of the King's Royal Regiment of New York and other corps; the names of all those who drew lands in the counties of Stormont, Dundas and Glengarry up to November*

1786; and several other lists of interest to the descendants of the old settlers. Cornwall: Standard Printing House, 1890. 421pp.

The most basic book of historical reference for this area, whose magnificent title says it all. A reprint by Mika was published in 1972 and a microfiche edition by CIHM in 1981. An *Index* of names, compiled by Lyall Manson, was published by the Stormont, Dundas and Glengarry Historical Society in 1975.

Diane Snyder Ptak. *The American loyalist: origins and nominal lists.* Albany, NY : D.S.Ptak, 1993. 34 leaves.

A brief description of Loyalist movements (which might serve as an introduction to novices), and an extensive bibliography covering the 13 American colonies and 6 Canadian ones. A useful tool to point the way to further reading.

Robert J. Quintin. *Guide to the Catholic parishes of the province of Ontario.* Pawtucket, R.I.: Quintin Publications, 1994. 64pp.

Roman Catholic churches listed by date of foundation, by town, by patron saint and alphabetically. Useful for determining which church's records might contain your ancestors.

Alan Rayburn. *Lost names and places of eastern Ontario.* Toronto: Ontario Genealogical Society, 1993. 50pp. ISBN: 1-55116-926-6.

Material from the twelve easternmost counties.

G. Elmore Reaman. *The trail of the black walnut.* Scottdale, Pa.: Herald Press, 1957. 256pp. Index.

Despite the decline in Reaman's reputation in recent years, this book remains significant for those interested in Pennsylvania-German settlements in Ontario. A revised edition was published by McClelland and Stewart in 1965 and a new edition by Genealogical Publishing in 1993.

A record of service: a guide to holdings of the Central Archives of the United Church of Canada. Toronto: United Church of Canada/Victoria University Archives, 1992. xii,391pp. Index.

Listing of denominational records and personal papers, but *individual congregational records are not included.* There is no guide for these records as yet. Available also in microfiche at half the price.

William D. Reid. ***Death notices of Ontario.*** Lambertville, N.J.: Hunterdon House, 1980. 417pp. ISBN: 0-912606-06-1. Indexed.
    Extracted from many periodicals covering the period 1810-1849. Full text not necessarily given. Other death notices extracted by Reid published in v.5 of *Ontario Register* (q.v.). Companion volume to his *Marriage notices of Ontario.*

William D. Reid. ***Marriage notices of Ontario.*** Lambertville, N.J.: Hunterdon House, 1980. 550pp. ISBN: 0-912606-05-3. Indexed.
    Extracts from many periodicals 1813-1854. Index of 16,000 names. Supplemented by Thomas B. Wilson's *Ontario Marriage Notices* (q.v.). Originals of these and the death notices are at the Weldon library, University of Western Ontario.

W.G. Reive. ***Cemeteries and graves in the Niagara district, Ontario.*** St. Catharines: D. Robbins, 1991. 476pp. ISBN: 1-895473-01-2. Index.
    Originals at the Archives of Ontario and available on microfilm. Dr. Reive transcribed many cemeteries in the 1920s and 1930s; the stones he saw may have vanished by the time later transcriptions were done.

Verna Ronnow. ***Inventory of cemeteries in Ontario.*** Toronto: Ontario Genealogical Society, 1987. 248pp.
    Every known cemetery (as of 1987), with location and whether transcribed at that time. Although there have been changes, it remains the best resource for finding a cemetery in the province. A vital reference tool. Supersedes the much smaller 1983 edition, which should now be regarded as unreliable.

Renie A. Rumpel. ***Index to marriage registrations of Ontario, Canada, 1869-1873.*** Waterloo: Ontario Indexing Services, 1995-96. 6 v. ISBN: 0-9699238-1-3 (book 2).
    Re-indexing using the original registrations, all names. This is meant to supersede the official handwritten (and difficult) index.

Dorothy E. Ryder. ***Checklist of Canadian directories, 1790-1950.*** Ottawa: National Library of Canada, 1979. xvii,290pp. ISBN: 0-660-50409-X. Bibliography.
    Superseded by Bond (q.v.)

J.E. Sanderson. ***The first century of Methodism in Canada.*** Toronto: William Briggs, 1908. 2v.

    Despite its all-embracing title, it does have references to individual 'stations' which may assist researchers in determining if there was a Methodist preacher in your area when your family was there. The anecdotes and photographs may also provide material for a family history.

Jack I. Schecter. ***Guide to the holdings of the Upper Canada Village Reference Library and Archives for family history researchers.*** Morrisburg: Upper Canada Village, 1995. 40pp.

    An unusual location, but rich in materials for the surrounding area, especially Dundas and Stormont counties, and welcoming to family historians.

Neil Semple. ***Genealogical resources at the United Church Archives.*** Kingston: Kingston branch OGS, 1985. 5pp.

    Very brief and now somewhat old, this remains a useful introduction to the subject.

Catherine Shepard. ***Surrogate court records at the Archives of Ontario.*** Toronto: Ontario Genealogical Society, 1984. 23pp. ISBN: 0-920036-05-8.

    A very brief introduction, but contains listings of all jurisdictions and years of holdings.

William H. Smith. ***Smith's Canadian gazetteer comprising statistical and general information respecting all parts of the upper province, or Canada West.*** Toronto: H.& W. Rowsell, 1846. 285pp., map.

    Various later editions. The brief descriptions of settlements make useful additions to family histories.

Southern Ontario maps, 1747 (Indian) to 1974. Hamilton: Hamilton branch OGS, 1985. unpaged.

    Maps drawn by Frances Walker from various originals. Most useful for researchers are those showing development of the various districts before 1850.

Corlene Taylor & Maggie Parnall. ***Mini-atlas of early settlers in the district of Niagara, 1782 to 1876.*** Beamsville: C.Taylor, 1991 (fifth printing, revised). unpaged. ISBN: 0-9691585-1-3.

A collection of local maps, some photocopied and some redrawn, from assorted sources. Many contain people's names.

Ryan Taylor. *Important genealogical collections in Ontario libraries and archives: a directory.* Toronto: Ontario Genealogical Society, 1994. 75pp. ISBN: 0-7779-0185-4.

A guide for those making genealogical research visits, detailing scope of collections and rules for researchers.

Mary Kearns Trace. *Guide to southern Ontario place names for family researchers.* Calgary, AB: Traces, 1986. unpaged, maps. ISBN: 0-921337-08-6.

A "take-along guide" with small maps showing the townships, and an alphabetical index, with references to the historical atlas series. This is a handy reference tool.

Upper Canada gleanings. Ayr: A. Gordon Keys, 1990- . (in progress) ISSN: 0847-2319.

Volumes 1-11 are all extractions of information about liquor licenses before 1841, with references to the original documents. This includes innkeepers, distillers and shops. The volumes are divided by district.

Dan Walker & Robert W. Calder. *The marriage registers of Upper Canada.* Delhi: NorSim Research, 1995-

These are the district marriage registers, which record weddings from the 1830s to the 1850s. Walker's transcriptions provide names of all participants and date. The early volumes are mostly from western Ontario (Talbot, Huron, London), but include Bathurst, with Newcastle forthcoming.

Russ Waller. *U.E. Loyalist links.* Kingston: R.Waller, 1993-1994. Rev. ed. 3 v., maps. Index.

Data on Loyalist families from many sources, coordinated in genealogies covering the first century in Canada. V. 1 concerns Frontenac county, v.2 Lennox & Addington, v.3, Prince Edward and Hastings.

Loral and Mildred Wanamaker. *1800-1841 Presbyterian register of Rev. Robert James McDowall.* Kingston: Kingston branch OGS, 1980. 92pp., map. Index.

Extractions from the original registers, previously transcribed in the OHS *Papers and records* v. 1 (1899), but with errors. McDowall's work was principally in Prince Edward, Lennox & Addington, and Frontenac counties.

War services of Canadian Knights of Columbus, 1939-1947. 260pp., illus.

Mainly focusing on the charitable work in Britain. Other lodges or fraternal organizations may also have publications detailing members' war work.

Wilfred D. Warner. *The accounts ledger, Niagara circuit Methodists, 1795-1823.* s.l.: s.n., n.d. 192pp., illus.

An unusual resource: a photocopied ledger, with typewritten explanations of the entries, and supplementary material. A great deal of data, but difficult to digest.

Emily P. Weaver. *The story of the counties of Ontario.* Toronto: Bell & Cockburn, 1913. 318pp. Index.

Brief early histories, including the northern districts. Useful for background and color.

Wesleyan Methodist baptismal register. Toronto: United Church of Canada Archives, 1990. 53pp.

This is their "Finding Aid #30", the guide to Fonds #5/8, the Wesleyan Methodist central registers. The registers are generally available on four microfilms, but this paper guide can be useful in knowing which pages to consult for particular townships. It may not be as generally accessible. The Archives has also issued updates or corrections. There are many published volumes of extractions from these records, which are listed in this bibliography under the area concerned. Researchers using this material should remember that baptisms are registered at the place of residence of the clergyman, not the baby.

Donald Whyte. *A dictionary of Scottish emigrants to Canada before Confederation.* Toronto: Ontario Genealogical Society, 1986. 443pp. ISBN: 0-920036-09-0. Extensive bibliography.

Dictionary-style entries of 12,500 people, plus their children, giving names, places, dates, relationships. Extracted from a wide variety of sources (all given). Supplement due to appear in 1996.

Bruce G. Wilson and Anita Burdett. *Manuscripts and government records in the United Kingdom and Ireland relating to Canada.* Ottawa: National Archives of Canada, 1992. xxxi,705pp. ISBN: 0-660-57424-1. Indexes.
    Extensive listings including itemisation of individual documents in repositories throughout Britain and Ireland. Access ensured through a detailed subject index and place index. If the original material has been microfilmed and made available at the NAC, call numbers are given. A good sourcebook for those searching for information on British regiments who served in Canada. A great deal of pre-1850 material.

Thomas B. Wilson. *Directory of the province of Ontario, 1857, with a gazetteer.* Lambertville, N.J.: Hunterdon House, 1987. ix,712pp.

Thomas B. Wilson. *Marriage bonds of Ontario, 1803-1834.* Lambertville, N.J.: Hunterdon House, 1985. 445pp. ISBN: 0-912606-26-6. Indexed.
    From originals at the National Archives of Canada, available on microfilm. Good introduction.

Thomas B. Wilson. *Ontario marriage notices.* Lambertville, N.J.: Hunterdon House, 1982. 435pp. ISBN: 0-912606-07-X. Indexed.
    "Complements and supplements the late William D. Reid's *Marriage notices of Ontario.*" (q.v.) Extractions from *The Christian Guardian, The Constitution* and *The Church.* Examine introduction carefully before using.

Joan Winearls. *Mapping Upper Canada, 1780-1867: an annotated bibliography of manuscript and printed maps.* Toronto: University of Toronto Press, 1991. xli,986pp., illus. Bibliography. Index.
    The definitive word on this subject, by the acknowledged authority. Consult it to see what maps exist of your ancestors' area when they lived there.

William R. Yeager. *Wills of the London district, 1800-1839, London District Surrogate Registry.* Simcoe: Norfolk Historical Society, 1979. 34pp. Index.
Abstract and index.

A.H. Young. *The war book of Upper Canada College, Toronto.* Toronto: Printers Guild, 1923. 322pp., ports.
Portraits and biographies of all UCC Old Boys who served in World War I, with details of service. This sort of publication was common after WWI (less so after WWII) for schools, universities, clubs and businesses. They may provide a potted biography of a relation.

Bill Zuefelt. *Court of probate registers and estate files at the Archives of Ontario (1793-1859).* Toronto: Ontario Genealogical Society, 1986. 43pp. ISBN: 0-920036-13-9.
The Court of Probate had provincial jurisdiction, while the surrogate courts had county jurisdictions. This book deals only with estates registered in the Court of Probate.

Algoma District

Cemeteries in Algoma are published by Sault Ste Marie & district branch OGS. SEE ALSO note under Rainy River District.

Joseph & Estelle Bayliss. *Historic St. Joseph Island.* Cedar Rapids, Iowa : Torch Press, 1938. 237pp., illus. Indexed.
The site of a fort and battles in the war of 1812. Early settler information included in later chapters.

The Bruce Mines Spectator, index of birth, death & marriage notices. Sault Ste. Marie: Sault and District branch OGS, 1987 2 v.
Done in the form of a computerized chart; page in the paper is included. Years covered are 1901-1956.

Edith M. Cameron. *Pioneers in a land of promise.* Iron Bridge: E.M.Cameron, 1993. 276pp., illus.
A history of Bright and Day townships, with many lists of names and biographies.

W. Allison Dempsey. *Growing up on the...* SEE UNDER Russell County

Iris Elliott & Margaret MacTavish. ***Wesleyan Methodist baptismal records for the district of Algoma.*** Sault Ste Marie: Saulte Ste Marie & District branch OGS, 1988. various pagings.
Extractions from the microfilmed originals at the United Church Archives.

Julien Hamelin & Narcisse Courchesne. *Moyen-Nord Ontarien.* SEE UNDER Sudbury District.

Frances Heath. ***Index to the 1861 census of Ontario, Algoma district.*** Sault Ste Marie & District branch OGS, 1987. various pagings. ISBN: 1-55075-107-7.
Every name alphabetical index with full entry, but no family groupings. Useful introduction.

Index of birth, marriage and death notices from the Sault Daily Star... Sault Ste. Marie: Sault and district branch, Ontario Genealogical Society, n.d. (in progress)
Indexes with brief entries only. Vols. 1-4 cover 1901-1925.

Index to Algoma wills, 1859 to 1928. Sault Ste Marie: Sault and district branch, Ontario Genealogical Society, n.d. unpaged.
Principal names only, with file numbers.

Carl Kauffmann. ***Logging days in Blind River.*** Blind River: C.Kauffmann, 1970. 146pp., illus.

Lorne W. Main. ***Index to 1881 Canadian census of Northwest territories and Algoma, Ontario.*** Vancouver: Main, 1984. 105pp., maps. ISBN: 0-9691093-3-4.
Heads of families and strays index.

J.R. Middleton. ***The white rapids: a history of the founding of Sault Ste. Marie.*** s.l.: s.n., n.d. 35pp., illus. Bibliography.

Brant County

Cemeteries in Brant are published by Brant County branch OGS.

Brant county: a directory of genealogical sources and resources.
Brantford: Brant County branch OGS, 1992. 32pp., maps. ISBN: 1-55116-506-6.
    A fine brief guide, including extensive bibliographical references, addresses and descriptions of repositories. Can be used in conjunction with Files, *Tracing your family...* (q.v.)

Brant county directories, farmers' 1885. Brantford: Brant County branch OGS, 1987. unpaged.
    Photocopied pages from a larger directory for several counties.

Burford, Fairfield Plains and area Methodist and United church.
Brantford: Brant County branch OGS, n.d. 4v.
    Church records: Baptisms 1900-1940 (gaps; ISBN: 1-55116-127-3); Marriages 1896-1941; Marriages 1898-1941 (ISBN: 1-55116-122-2); Burials 1902-1940 (gaps), (ISBN: 1-55116-123-0).

Cainsville United Church, baptismal register, 1937-1954; burial register, 1937-1957. Brantford: Brant County branch OGS, 1981. 12 leaves.
    Names, parents, birthplace, birthdate and place for baptisms; name, place, age, deathdate, cause and burial place for burials. The branch also published volumes of *Marriages 1936-1958* (1981), *Marriages 1897-1919* (1981) and *Marriages 1858-1869* (1982).

Farmers' directory for the county of Brant ca. 1891. Brantford: Brant County branch OGS, 1981. 3v.
    Photocopied sheets from an old directory, one volume for Brantford, one for Burford, one for S.Dumfries, Oakland and Onondaga.

Angela Files & Gary Sheldrick. ***Church directory for the county of Brant.*** Brantford: Brant County branch OGS, 1985. 24pp.
    Now somewhat outdated, and the addresses lack postal codes, but may be used as a guide in the second step of locating church records (keeping in mind its limitations).

Angela Files. *The early development of municipal government in Brant county.* Brantford: Brant County branch OGS, 1985? 18pp.
    Consists mostly of lists of politicians with years of office.

Angela Files. *First Congregational Church, Brantford, Ontario, church register.* Brantford: Brant County branch OGS, 1990. 6 v.
    The volumes include: officers and members, 1864, baptisms and members, 1840 to 1848; debating minutes 1899 to 1901; membership 1853-1910; business meetings, 1853-1891; church history (a republication of John Robertson's *History of the Brantford Congregational Church, 1820 to 1920).*

Angela Files. *The marriage licenses issued at Brantford by William Richardson 1838 to 1839.* Brantford: Brant County branch OGS, 1987. 6pp.
    Names, date, names of sureties.

Angela Files. *The original land patentees of Burford and Oakland townships.* Brantford: Brant County branch OGS, 1983. 10pp.
    Name, date and location, but no source.

Angela Files. *St. Matthew's Lutheran church book, 1904-1940's, Brantford, Ontario.* Brantford: Brant County Branch OGS, 1990. 122 leaves.
    Includes baptisms, communicants, marriages, confirmations, burials, other records; no index.

Angela Files. *Tracing your family in Brant county.* Brantford: Brant County branch OGS. 92pp. ISBN: 1-55116-158-3 (1990 reprint).
    One of the earliest county handbooks, now outdated in many ways but still useful in its historical aspects. Should be used in conjunction with *Brant County: a directory...* (q.v.)

Glen Morris United Church register of baptisms 1853. Brantford: Brant County branch OGS, n.d. unpaged. ISBN: 1-55116-148-6.
    This volume is awkwardly titled, for it covers 1853-1878. The church was, at that time, Presbyterian (in South Dumfries township). The branch has also published other records, including four volumes of

communion rolls and disjunctions (1853-1918), and marriages (1853-1857) and burials (1853-1884).

Grace Anglican Church, Brantford, Ontario. Brantford: Brant County branch OGS, 1987. 7v. Indexes.
>Church records: Marriages 1827-1904. V.7 is an overall index.

History of the county of Brant, Ontario.... Toronto: Warner, Beers, 1883. 687pp.
>Substantial section of biographical sketches. Index by D. Alan Young without publisher's name or date.

Illustrated historical atlas of Brant county, Ontario. Belleville: Mika, 1972. xix,59pp., illus. ISBN: 0-919302-25-4.
>Originally published by Page & Smith, Toronto, 1875. Includes maps with names.

Index of Tremaine's map of the county of Brant, Canada West, 1858. Brantford: Brant County branch OGS, 1981. 15pp., map.
>Transcription of an earlier, undated index. Map included. Tremaine's oversize wall maps included names of plot owners, churches, cemeteries and town plans.

C.M. Johnston. ***Brant county, a history 1784-1945.*** Toronto: Oxford University Press, 1967. 181pp. Bibliographical references. Index.

A list of members shown on the books of First Baptist Church, Brantford, from 1853-1884 taken from the book Jubilee Review of First Baptist Church, Brantford, 1833-1884. Brantford: Brant County branch OGS, n.d. 28, 14pp.
>Reprinting of the *Jubilee Review* first published in 1890; the branch also published a membership list for 1884-1914. Includes information about where members came from and where they went.

Janice J. Miller. ***1851 Brant county census index.*** Vernon, MI: J.J.Miller, 1985. 184pp.
>Heads of family index.

Mohawk Chapel. Brantford: Brant County branch OGS, 1991. 5v. Index.

A history and records of Her Majesty's Chapel of the Mohawks, Brantford, (Anglican), including baptisms (1827-1840s); marriages (1827-1877); burials (1829-1947).

The Oxford-Waterloo papers...
Includes material from the Paris *Star.* SEE UNDER Waterloo County

F. Douglass Reville. *History of the county of Brant.* Brantford: Hurley Printing, 1920. 2 v., illus.
Many anecdotes; large military section with lists.

Gloria J. Scott. *Births & deaths, 1852-1857, the Brantford Conservative.* Brantford: Brant County branch OGS, 1990. unpaged. ISBN: 1-55116-157-5.
Name and date only, in computer index format.

James Sutherland. *County of Brant gazetteer and directory, 1869-70.* Brantford: Brant County branch OGS, 1983. 81pp.
Originally published in Toronto, 1869.

Mike Wingrove. *Voters' list, 1847, town of Brantford.* Brantford: Brant County branch OGS, 1984. 2pp.

Bruce County

Cemeteries in Bruce are published by Bruce & Grey branch OGS.

Births, deaths & marriages from the Paisley advocate (a weekly newspaper). Port Elgin: Bruce County Genealogical Society, 1990-1991. 3v. ISBN: 1-895117-00-3 (v.1) Index.
v.1: 1871-1900; v.2: 1901-1910; v.3: 1911-1920. Full text not given.

Dorothy Crocker. *Albemarle, a history of the township.* Wiarton: Albemarle Township Historical Society, 1991. 339pp., illus. ISBN: 0-9695680-0-2.

School pictures, soldiers. Community and location histories include much family information.

1851 census, Bruce county, Ontario, Canada. Port Elgin: Bruce County Genealogical Society, 1993. 4 v. ISBN: 1-895117-03-8 (Arran & Elderslie)
  Full transcription. Volumes published so far are: Arran & Elderslie; Brant; Kinloss & Greenock; Bruce & Saugeen.

1867 directory of the county of Bruce, Canada West. Montreal: J.W. Rooklidge, 1867. 211pp.
  More generally available in the Bruce branch OGS reprint of 1972.

Wanita Hollands Fletcher. *Toil, tears, & triumph: a history of Kincardine township.* Kincardine: Kincardine Township Historical Society, 1990. 439pp., illus. ISBN: 0-929783-94-5. Index.
  Lot-by-lot summary of family histories.

Josephine Elizabeth Hahn. *Home of my youth: Hanover.* Privately published. 298pp.
  More far-ranging than the title suggests, with church histories and recollections of individuals in the late 19th century.

Gwen Smith Harrison. *Families and farms of Huron township with its hub, Ripley.* Ripley: Ripley-Huron Reunion 1985 Historical Committee, 1985. 399pp., illus. ISBN: 0-9692040-0-0. Index.
  Largely genealogies. The township history books of Bruce and Grey counties tend to be heavily genealogical and should be sought out.

Illustrated historical atlas of counties Grey & Bruce, Ont. Port Elgin: Cummings, 1975. 124pp., illus.
  Originally published by Belden, Toronto, 1880. Includes maps with names and directories originally published elsewhere.

Norman McLeod. *The history of the county of Bruce, and the minor municipalities therein, 1907-1968.* Owen Sound: Bruce County Historical Society, 1969. x,477pp., illus. Indexed.
  Companion volume to Robertson.

Norman Robertson. *The history of the county of Bruce, and of the minor municipalities therein.* Toronto: Wm. Briggs, 1906. 560pp., illus. Indexed.
   For 20th century material, see McLeod.

St. Andrew's church, Saugeen township & North Bruce church, Bruce township, baptism records, 1872-1918. Port Elgin: Bruce County Genealogical Society, 1995. 11 leaves. ISBN: 1-895117-09-7.
   Full information in a computerized format. Original Presbyterian records now at the United Church Archives in Toronto.

Clayton Schaus. *The Chesley district.* Chesley?: s.n., 1967. 100pp., illus.
   Anecdotal history, including Chesley and Elderslie, with many names.

Betty Warrilow. *Tracing your ancestors in Bruce and Grey.* Owen Sound: Bruce & Grey branch OGS, 1993. Rev. ed. 82pp. Index.
   Rich in addresses and bibliographical references. Originally published 1976, with revised editions in 1982 and 1988.

Carleton County
   Cemeteries in Carleton are published by Ottawa branch OGS.

Eve Beauregard-Malak & Marthe Faribault-Beauregard. *Répertoire des sépultures de Notre-Dame-de-Lourdes, Vanier & Saint-Joseph, Orléans.* Ottawa: Centre de généalogie S.C., 1983. 426pp., maps.
   These are Roman Catholic parishes. Until 1967, Vanier was known as Eastview.

Beechwood cemetery interment registry index, 1931-1955. Ottawa: Ottawa branch OGS, 1995. 237pp. ISBN: 1-55116-735-2.
   Index to the records, not tombstones. "This is an index and does not contain all of the information available..." The originals are at the Ottawa City Archives. The branch has also published the interment register for *1901-1930* (1993; ISBN: 1-55116-730-1) and the earlier *Burial Records of Beechwood Cemetery, 1873-1900* (1991; ISBN: 1-55034-8957).

The Bytown Gazette. Stratford: Bur-Mor, 1992- . (in progess) ISBN: 1-55024-145-1 (v.1) Index.

Extracts from the newspapers, published in Ottawa, chiefly births, deaths and marriages, texts given in full. The first volume includes material from the *Bytown Independent.* Volumes 1-3 cover 1836 to 1845.

Tom Carmody & Bruce Elliott. *Wesleyan Methodist baptisms, Bytown/Ottawa, nineteenth century.* Ottawa: Ottawa branch OGS, 1988. 18pp.
Extracted from microfilm at the United Church Archives in Toronto by Bruce Elliott and published in *Ottawa Branch News.* Tom Carmody collected and indexed them. Since 1988, more have been published in the branch newsletter.

Jean-Paul Delisle & Denis Ouimet. *Baptêmes, mariages et sépultures de la paroisse La Nativité de Notre-Seigneur Jésus-Christ, Ottawa, Ontario, 1960-1987.* Ottawa: Société franco-ontarienne d'histoire et de généalogie, 1990. viii,93pp. ISSN: 0823-1575 (Paroisses de l'Ontario français). Index.
Vol. 24 in the series.

Marguerite Dufour, Madeleine Dumouchel, Julien Hamelin. *Répertoire de mariages, paroisse Saint-Joseph, Ottawa, 1856-1984.* Ottawa: Centre de généalogie S.C., 1985. 347pp. ISBN: 0-88662-078-3. Index.
Name, parents, date. "Répertoire no. 65."

Julien Hamelin. *Mariages de la paroisse Sacre-Coeur, Ottawa, 1889-1975.* Ottawa: Centre de généalogie S.C., n.d. pp.111-299. Index.
Names of participants, date and parents. Includes marriages in the chapel of the University of Ottawa.

Julien Hamelin. *Mariages de la paroisse Saint-Charles, 1908-1975, Ottawa & Vanier.* Ottawa: Centre de généalogie S.C., n.d. 107pp. Index.
Names, parents, date. "Répertoire no. 1A."

Julien Hamelin. *Répertoire des mariages de la paroisse Sainte-Brigide, Ottawa, 1889-1982.* Ottawa: Centre de généalogie S.C., 1984. 184pp. Index.
Name, parents, date. "Publication no. 49."

Historical sketch of the county of Carleton. Belleville: Mika, 1971. 354pp. ISBN: 919302-12-2. Index.
    Originally published by Belden in 1879 as the lengthy introduction to the *Illustrated historical atlas* (below). This edition has a personal names index.

Illustrated historical atlas of the county of Carleton (including city of Ottawa), Ont. Port Elgin: Ross Cumming, 1971. 1v,48pp., maps.
    Originally published by Belden in 1879. The township maps include names.

Gilles Joly. *Répertoire des mariages de la paroisse Sainte-Anne d'Ottawa, 1873-1980.* Ottawa: Centre de généalogie S.C., 1980. 167pp. Index.
    Names, parents and date. "Publication no. 15."

Michel Langlois. *Répertoire des mariages de Saint-François d'Assise d'Ottawa (province d'Ontario) (1891-1964).* Quebec City: Société canadienne de généalogie (Québec), 1967. 196pp.
    This is a Roman Catholic parish. Includes names, date and parents' names.

Hector Lavergne et al. *Mariages, Notre-Dame-de-Lourdes de Cyrville (Ottawa), 1873-1985.* Ottawa: Société franco-ontarienne d'Histoire et de Généalogie, 1986. 130pp. (Series: Paroisses de l'Ontario français)
    Full entries under groom, index under bride. V. 12 in the series.

Norma Simpson Morrison. *Methodist marriages on the Metcalfe circuit, Ottawa district, Montreal conference, County of Carleton, Province of Ontario, 1902-1912, 1917-1923.* Vernon: Osgoode Township Historical Society, 1987. 15 leaves. Index.
    Full text. Originals at the United Church Archives, Montreal.

Léon Nadon. *Répertoire des mariages de Saint-Jean-Baptiste d'Ottawa (Ontario) (1872-1969).* Quebec City: Société canadienne de généalogie (Québec), 1970. 270pp.
    This is a Roman Catholic parish. Includes names, date and parents' names.

Michael & James Neelin. *1836-1845 Bytown Gazette, abstracts of births, deaths & marriages, Bytown Independent for 1836.* Ottawa: Ottawa branch OGS, 1979. unpaged. ISBN: 0-920036-98-8. Index.
    Full text.

Garfield Thomas Ogilvie. *Once upon a country lane: a tribute to the Gaelic spirit of old West Huntley, Carleton County, Ontario.* Nepean: House of Airlie, 1992. 386pp., illus.
    Much of the material is taken from the author's own experience; many names are mentioned.

Ottawa directory for 1874-75...to which are added directories of New Edinburgh, Hull, Aylmer, Chelsea, Gatineau Mills, Ironside, L'Original, Buckingham and the revised Voters' List of the County of Carleton. Ottawa: A.S.Woodburn, 1874. 288pp.

Jean-Yves Pelletier. *Baptêmes, mariages, sépultures de la paroisse Saint-Pie X, Ottawa, 1954-1984.* Ottawa: Centre de généalogie S.C., 1985. 108pp.
    Full information given. "Publication no. 71."

Répertoire des mariages de la cathédrale d'Ottawa, 1827-1980. Ottawa: Centre de généalogie S.C., 1983. 2 v.
    "Répertoire no. 38." Names, parents, date. This is the Roman Catholic cathedral.

Répertoire des mariages du comté Ottawa-Carleton (14 paroisses). Ottawa: Centre du généalogie S.C., 1986. 512pp.
    Names of participants & their parents, date, church. The parishes are all Roman Catholic.

Charles Roger. *Ottawa past and present: a brief account of the first opening up of the Ottawa country, and incidents in connection with the rise and progress of Ottawa city, and parts adjacent thereto.* Ottawa: Times Printing, 1871. 124pp.

Cochrane District

SEE ALSO note under Rainy River District.

Michael Barnes. ***Timmins, the porcupine country.*** Erin: Boston Mills Press, 1991. 144pp., illus. ISBN: 1-55046-050-1. Bibliography.

Julien Hamelin. ***Répertoire des mariages de Cochrane, la région avoisinante, 1883-1981.*** Ottawa: Centre de généalogie S.C., 1985. 413pp.
    Marriages from 13 churches, the earliest of which was founded in 1883 (Chapleau), scattered over a wide area in Cochrane and Sudbury districts. Names, parents, date.

Julien Hamelin. ***Répertoire des mariages de Kapuskasing & la région avoisinante, 1917-1981.*** Ottawa: Centre de généalogie S.C., 1985. 343pp. ISBN: 0088662-085-6. Index.
    Records from nine churches, mostly along Highway 11 near Kapuskasing. Names, parents and date. "Publication no. 70."

Julien Hamelin. ***Répertoire des mariages du diocèse de Timmins, 1905-1980.*** Ottawa: Centre de généalogie S.C., 1983. 3 v. Index.
    The Roman Catholic diocese of Timmins covers a wide area in the districts of Cochrane and Timiskaming; a list of the 38 parishes included is in each volume. Names, parents, date, parish.

Watson Kirkconnell. ***Kapuskasing, an historical sketch.*** Kingston: Queen's University Department of History and Political and Economic Science, 1921. 15pp.
    Issued as the department's *Bulletin* no. 38, January 1921.

Alice Marwick. ***Northland post.*** Cochrane: A.Marwick, 1950. 341pp., illus.
    A history of Cochrane and district.

Dufferin County

The publication of **Cemeteries** *in Dufferin is not the responsibility of any OGS branch; however, some are published by Waterloo-Wellington branch and Lois Black.*

Gary Bagley & Lynne Webb. ***Spring Valley cemetery, Horning's Mills, Lot 12, concession 1, Melancthon township, Dufferin county.*** s.l.: s.n., 1978? 9pp., map. Index.

Margaret Beettam. ***The Orangeville Sun, an index.*** Oakville: Halton-Peel branch OGS, 1993. 3 v. ISBN: 0-9693991-7-0 (v.1).
Index only: name, date of newspaper, type of event. Years covered are 1860-1899.

Alan Rayburn & Mary Rayburn. ***Gravestone inscriptions of Forest Lawn Cemetery, Orangeville, Ontario, to 1988.*** Nepean: Alan Rayburn Research Associates, 1989. 245pp., maps.
Available from Dufferin County Museum, along with his readings of Greenwood Cemetery, Orangeville and cemeteries in Mono.

Dundas County

Cemeteries of Dundas are available from Ottawa branch OGS.

J. Smyth Carter. ***The story of Dundas from 1784 to 1904.*** Belleville: Mika, 1973. 463pp., illus.
Originally published 1905.

James Croil. ***Dundas, or a sketch of Canadian history.*** Montreal: B.Dawson, 1861. 352pp. Indexed.

John Graham Harkness. *Stormont, Dundas & Glengarry...* SEE UNDER Stormont County.

Historical review of Winchester, Ont. Winchester: Old Home Reunion Committee, 1934. 48pp., illus.
Program for the reunion of 1934, with historical fragments.

Illustrated historical atlas of the counties of Stormont, Dundas and Glengarry, 1879; Prescott and Russell (supplement of the Illustrated Atlas of the Dominion of Canada 1881), H. Belden & Co., Toronto; H.F. Walling's map of the counties of Stormont, Dundas, Glengarry, Prescott and Russell (Canada West), 1862. Port Elgin: Cumming, 1972. 88pp., illus.

The original atlas published in Toronto by Belden, here teamed with part of the Canada atlas and a reduced version of the wall map (on which the names are difficult to read). The Stormont-Dundas-Glengarry atlas only was also reprinted by Mika (1972; ISBN: 0-919302-26-2).

Mildred R. & Edwin Livingston. *Pioneer Memorial cemetery transcriptions, Upper Canada Village, 1977.* Prescott: Livingston, 1977. 19,xviiipp. ISNB: 0-920992-17-X. Indexed.

Gravestones moved to Upper Canada Village from the flooded lands of the St. Lawrence Seaway. Useful in connection with Smart (q.v.)

Clive Marin & Frances Marin. *Stormont, Dundas and Glengarry, 1945-1978.* Belleville: Mika, 1982. 644pp., illus. ISBN: 0-929303-63-3. Indexed. Bibliography.

The bibliography is extensive and worth investigating.

Marriages, 1896-1968, Baptist Church, Ormond. Vernon: Osgoode Township Historical Society, n.d. 12 leaves. Index.

Full text.

James Smart. *Data on existing cemeteries in the United Counties of Dundas and Stormont affected by the St. Lawrence Power Project. Ontario-St. Lawrence Development Commission, 1956.* 190p.

Reprinted 1995 by the Upper Canada Village Reference Library. When the St. Lawrence Seaway was built, villages and cemeteries disappeared under the waters. This lists the tombstones on the eighteen cemeteries in Matilda, Williamsburg and Osnabruck townships which had to be moved.

Durham County

Cemeteries in Durham are published *by Kawartha branch and Whitby-Oshawa branch OGS.*

Dorothy Brown. *Index to map of township of Cavan surveyed by Sam: G. Wilmot 1817; original landowners compiled and drawn by W.C. Coulter 1980.* Whitby: Whitby-Oshawa branch OGS, n.d. 12pp.

Agnes Burley. *Clarke township, eastern section: its places, people & events.* Newtonville?: s.n., 1967. 120pp., illus.
    Most of the text is family histories, written in a colloquial manner. Despite its name, it includes families from all of Clarke and surrounding townships.

Isabelle Challice & Grant Curtis. *Spirit of the hills.* s.l.: s.n., n.d. 179pp., illus.
    History of the churches with United church connections in Manvers township (Methodist and Presbyterian). Available from Grant Curtis.

J.T. Coleman. *History of the early settlement of Bowmanville and vicinity.* Bowmanville: West Durham Steam Printing, 1875. 43p.
    Includes 1812 militia list for the village, and some marriages.

Early families of Port Hope and area. Port Hope: East Durham Historical Society, 1983- . (in progress) ISBN: 0-921072-10-4 (v.7).
    Brief family histories as submitted by researchers. Each volume contains a miscellaneous collection. As of 1995, there are 9 volumes.

Robert R. Halfyard. *Index to 1891 census, Clarke township, Durham county, Ontario.* St. Catharines: Halfyard Heritage, 1987. 12p. ISBN: 0-921971-00-1.
    Heads of families and strays index. In 1988, he published a similar index for *Manvers* (ISBN: 0-921971-01-X).

Robert R. Halfyard. *Index to Clarke township, 1878 Belden's atlas of Northumberland and Durham counties, Ontario.* St. Catharines: Halfyard Heritage, 1990. 10 leaves.

Robert R. Halfyard. *Marriage registers, Pontypool-Janetville circuit, Bible Christian & Methodist churches, 1879-1917.* St. Catharines: Halfyard Heritage, 1992. 22pp. Index.
    Full entries.

A.R. Hazelgrove. *Name and place index to Illustrated Historical Atlas of the counties of Northumberland and Durham, Ontario.* Kingston: Hazelgrove, 1976. 89pp.

Margaret Burns Hogan. *Echoes from the hills: a history of the community of Mount Pleasant, 1817-1987.* Cavan: Young & Hogan Publishing, 1988. 144pp., illus. ISBN: 0-921432-00-3. Index.
   This community is in Cavan township. The index is very sketchy.

Illustrated historical atlas of Northumberland and Durham counties, Ontario. Belleville: Mika, 1972. x,115pp., illus. ISBN: 0-919302-18-1.
   Originally published by Belden, Toronto, 1878. Includes maps with names. For *Index*, see under Hazelgrove and Halfyard, above.

Names listed on the 1861 Tremaine map of Durham county, Ontario. Whitby: Whitby-Oshawa branch OGS, n.d. 5v.
   Published in five parts: Cavan, Clarke, Darlington, Hope, Manvers. There is no published index for Cartwright. Rudimentary in format.

Alan E. Richards. *Darlington township index to the 1861 Tremaine map of Durham County, Ontario.* Whitby: Whitby-Oshawa branch OGS, n.d. 20pp.
   Name, lot, occupation.

Shirley Simons et al. *1861 census for Cartwright township in the county of Durham.* Whitby: Whitby-Oshawa branch OGS, n.d. 15pp. ISBN: 1-55114-254-6.
   Heads of families and strays.

John Squair. *The townships of Darlington and Clarke including Bowmanville and Newcastle.* Toronto: University of Toronto Press, 1927. 609pp. Indexed.
   Includes family histories.

Thelma Wright et al. *Index, 1851-52 census for Cartwright township in the county of Durham.* Whitby: Whitby-Oshawa branch OGS, n.d. 10pp. ISBN: 1-55114-252-X.
   Heads of families and strays only.

Elgin County

Cemeteries in Elgin are published by Elgin County branch OGS. The several items here listed with no publisher may be products of the Elgin County Library.

Jean Bircham & H. Mills. ***Index to Central Methodist (United) Church marriage register, 1896-1903.*** St. Thomas: Elgin County branch OGS, 1990. 16 leaves.

    Index only: name & page number, but all names in the records are indexed. No information is given as to the location of the records.

Jean Bircham. ***Index to crown patentees: Aldborough township.*** St. Thomas: Elgin County branch OGS, 1988. 13 leaves, map.

Jean Bircham. ***Index to crown patents: Dunwich township.*** St. Thomas: Elgin County branch OGS, 1988. 13 leaves, map.

Census index to 1851, Elgin county. St. Thomas: Elgin County Library, 1980-1984. 4 v.

    Families listed alphabetically, full transcription. The volumes are: Southwold, St. Thomas, Bayham, Malahide.

Census index to 1861, Elgin county. St. Thomas: Elgin County Library, 1981-1984. 6 v.

    Families listed alphabetically, full transcription. The volumes are: Southwold, St. Thomas, Vienna, Bayham, Dunwich, Malahide.

Frank Clarke. ***Documents relevant to landholding in Malahide township.*** s.l.: s.n., n.d. 95pp.

    For comment, see Yarmouth volume below.

Frank Clarke. ***Early township land papers: Yarmouth.*** s.l.: s.n., n.d. 214pp.

    This useful book may be difficult to find, as it has no publication information (as well as no index). It includes "pertinent information about Yarmouth" from the township papers at the Archives of Ontario.

James D. Curtis. ***St. Thomas and Elgin medical men of the past.*** St. Thomas: s.n, 1956. 122pp., ports.

Brief biographies and portraits of doctors; family information included.

Margaret Daugharty. *1873 Southwold collector's roll.* St. Thomas: Elgin County branch OGS, 1990. 28 leaves, map.
Tax records. Index only, for microfilm of originals at the Elgin County Library.

Margaret Daugharty. *Southwold assessment.* St. Thomas: Elgin County branch OGS, 1987-88. 4v.
Volumes for 1839, 1841, 1848, 1852. Index only, for orginals on microfilm at the Elgin County Library.

Maxwell F. Doan. *Index, New Sarum, Elgin county, Baptist church marriage registers, 1858-1975.* St. Thomas: Elgin County branch OGS, 1989. various pagings.
For v.1 (earliest marriages), full details are given. For the rest (1901 on), it is an index only. New Sarum church is at Aylmer.

Elgin county marriage register 1853-1857. s.l.: s.n., n.d. 2v. Index.
Transcriptions of the original registrations from the period immediately preceding the 1858 attempt at civil registration of marriages. Rare and useful material.

Elgin county marriage register 1869-1873. s.l.: s.n., n.d. 4v. Index.
Transcriptions of the original marriage registrations (official copies now at the Archives of Ontario).

Elgin county, Ontario, clerk of the peace, deaths register, 1869-1873. s.l.: s.n., n.d. 2v. Index.
Transcriptions of the original death registrations (official copies now at the Archives of Ontario).

Evenden Funeral Home and furniture store, index, 1873-1880. St. Thomas: Elgin County branch OGS, 1988. 21 leaves.
This funeral home was in St. Thomas. Name, date and index page only; full information is available from the branch.

Kay Fowler & Jean Bircham. *Marriages and index to Rev. D.W. Rowland marriage register, 1858-1890.* St. Thomas: Elgin County branch OGS, 1993. 71, 74pp. ISBN: 1-5504-696-2. Index.

 Rowland was a Baptist minister in St. Thomas. Full entries and every name index.

The Haggan papers. St. Thomas: Elgin County Library Board, 1978. 6 v.

 Genealogies and local history from papers in the estate of Ida Louise Haggan, now the property of the library. A treasure trove.

Historical sketches of the county of Elgin. St. Thomas: Elgin Historical and Scientific Institute, 1895. various pagings, illus.

 Very early history, rather dry.

Illustrated historical atlas of the county of Elgin, Ont. Port Elgin: Cumming, 1972. xxviii,58pp., illus.

 Originally published by Page, Toronto, 1877. Includes maps with names.

Index to 1842 census, Elgin county. St. Thomas: Elgin County Library, 1981. 4 v.

 The census was heads of families only; the index is alphabetical. The volumes are: Aldborough, Bayham, Malahide, Yarmouth.

An index to the deaths reported in the Aylmer Express between December 12, 1890 and August 22, 1907. s.l.: s.n., n.d. 305pp.

 Alphabetical, in computerized format. Name, date; possibly age, maiden name, other names, cause of death.

An index to the marriages reported in the Aylmer Express between December 12, 1890 and August 22, 1907. s.l.: s.n., n.d. 2v.

 Names of participants and date of entry in the newspaper only.

Robert A. Jones. *Methodist church baptismal records, 1840-1894 for Elgin county and North Dorchester township, Middlesex county.* St. Thomas: Elgin County branch OGS, 1991. 91pp. ISBN: 1-55034-690-3.

 Extracts from the Wesleyan central registers at the United Church Archives, Toronto.

James L. McCallum & Anne Daugharty. *Register of Reverend Caleb Burdick, index.* St. Thomas: Elgin County branch OGS, n.d. 21 leaves.
> Marriages 1833-1839; baptisms, 1822-1846; burials 1829-1844. Burdick was a Methodist operating in Malahide township. This is a rudimentary index only. The original register is at the United Church Archives, Toronto.

Moedinger Funeral Home, Sparta, Ontario, index, c1899-c1911. St. Thomas: Elgin County branch OGS, 1994. 5pp. ISBN: 1-55034-704-7.
> Name, date and cemetery.

Stephen J. Peters & Edward Phelps. *Wills of Elgin county, a selection, 1846-1852.* St. Thomas: Elgin County Public Library, 1983. 111pp.
> Originally published as part of the library's 1982 annual report. Republished under its own name, 1984.

Janice Faulkner Rezar. *Index of P.R. Williams & Sons Funeral Home records, 1893-1910.* St. Thomas: Elgin County branch OGS, 1986. 75 leaves.
> Name, cemetery and index page. The funeral home was in St. Thomas. Full information is available from the branch.

Janice Faulkner Rezar. *Malahide township vital statistics, 1890-1915.* St. Thomas: Elgin County branch OGS, 1987. 225pp.
> Full entries. Location of originals not stated.

Howard R. Rokeby-Thomas. *Church in the valley: Christ Church, Port Stanley, Ontario, Canada.* Port Stanley: Christ Church, 1949. 94pp., illus.
> Church history, but including transcriptions of the registers from 1872.

Marvin Ryder. *1881 index to census.* St. Thomas: Elgin County branch OGS. 11 v.
> Originally produced 1991-1993 at McMaster University by the author, later published more widely by the branch. Alphabetical.

Marvin Ryder. *1891 index to census.* St. Thomas: Elgin County branch OGS. 12 v.

Originally produced 1991-1993 at McMaster University by the author, later published more widely by the branch. Alphabetical.

The St. Thomas Weekly Dispatch. Stratford: Bur-Mor, 1988- (in progress) ISBN: 1-55024-051-X (v.1). Indexed.

Extracts from the newspaper, mostly BDMs, given in full. The first volume includes the *St. Thomas, Port Stanley & County of Elgin Advertiser.* Vols. 1-3 cover 1853-1863. In addition to this ongoing series, Bur-Mor has published three small volumes of newspaper extracts for short-lived papers in this area: *St. Thomas Liberal* (1832-1833); *The St. Thomas Standard* (1844-1846) and a composite volume for six papers (1832-1854).

Hugh Joffre Sims. *Sims' history of Elgin county.* St. Thomas: Elgin County Library, 1984. 3v., illus.

Arranged alphabetically by locality, with substantial entries for each place. This work reflects a lifetime's work collecting local history.

Tweedsmuir history, 1947 Women's Institute, West Lorne. s.l.: s.n., 1947? 1 v. (unpaged)

Few of the Tweedsmuir histories from around the province are published in book form; it is unfortunate that this one reveals so little of its publishing origins. However, for those with West Lorne ancestry, it is very interesting. A few other printed Tweedsmuirs may be found (such as that for Brooke township, Lambton County) but most are either in manuscript or on microfilm. See the introduction for more information.

Essex County

Cemeteries in Essex are published by Essex County branch OGS.

Pauline Bacon et al. ***Mariages et sépultures, paroisse Sainte-Anne, Tecumseh, 1859-1985.*** Ottawa: Société franco-ontarienne d'Histoire et de Généalogie, 1986. 399,137pp. plus supplement. ISSN: 0823-1575 (Paroisses de l'Ontario français) Index.

Vol. 14 in the series. Later marriages include place of baptism and birthdate. Marriages include parents and date.

Pauline Bacon et al. *Mariages et sépultures, paroisse St-Simon et St-Jude, Belle-Rivière, 1840-1985.* Ottawa: Société franco-ontarienne d'Histoire et de Généalogie, 1986. 339pp. ISSN: 0823-1575 (Paroisses de l'Ontario français).
    Vol. 11 in the series.

Births, marriages and deaths in Essex county, Ontario, as originally published in the Amherstburg Echo, November 1874-December 1876. Amherstburg: The Echo, 1984. 64pp.
    Full text. This volume and 1883 (below) were the only two issued in this series.

Lise Brûlé et al. *Baptêmes, paroisse l'Annonciation de Pointe-aux-Roches, 1867-1946.* Ottawa: Société franco-ontarienne d'Histoire et de Généalogie, 1985. 266pp. ISSN: 0823-1575 (Paroisses de l'Ontario français).
    Volume 10 in the series. Name, parents and date.

Lise Brûlé, Germaine Chiasson, Catherine St-Pierre. *Mariages & sépultures, L'Annonciation de Pointe-aux-Roches, Ont., 1867 à 1983.* Ottawa: Société franco-ontarienne d'Histoire et de Généalogie, 1984. various pagings. ISSN: 0823-1575 (Paroisses de l'Ontario français).
    Volume 5 in the series.

Lise Brûlé & Germaine Chiasson. *Mariages et sépultures, paroisse Saint-Joachim, 1882-1982.* Ottawa: Société franco-ontarienne d'Histoire et de Généalogie, 1984. various pagings. ISSN: 0823-1575 (Paroisses de l'Ontario français)
    Volume 3 in the series. Full text.

Germaine Chiasson et al. *Mariages, paroisse L'Assomption de Windsor, Ontario, 1700-1985.* Ottawa: Société franco-ontarienne d'Histoire et de Généalogie, 1985. 2 v. ISSN: 0823-1575 (Paroisses de l'Ontario français).
    The pair constitute no. 2 in the series.

Commemorative biographical record of the county of Essex, Ontario. Toronto: J.H. Beers, 1905. 676pp., ports.
    Biographies of "prominent and representative citizens", with historical sketches of early families.

Madeleine Dumouchel. *French pioneers of the Western District.* Toronto: Council for Franco-Ontarian Affairs, 1979. 90,90pp.
 Text identical in French and English. Brief history, family names with origins, brief genealogies.

1883 births marriages and deaths in Essex county, Ontario, as originally published in the Amherstburg Echo. Amherstburg: The Echo, 1984. various pagings.
 Full text.

50 years, 1921-1971, Tecumseh, Ont. Tecumseh: s.n., 1971. 47pp.

Illustrated historical atlas of the counties of Essex and Kent. Port Elgin: Cumming, 1973. 112pp., illus.
 Originally published by Belden, Toronto, 1881. Includes maps with names. For *Index*, see Pineau, below.

C.C. James. *Early history of the town of Amherstburg; a short, concise and interesting sketch.* Amherstburg: The Echo, 1902. 23pp.

The marriage records of Essex county, 1858-1864. Windsor: Essex County branch OGS, 1993. 94pp. Index.
 Full text of the ledgers at the Archives of Ontario, with an index.

Lisa Paquette, Jack Ramieri & Jenny Varga. *How to trace your roots in Essex county: a source guide.* Windsor: Windsor Public Library, 1984. 45pp. ISBN: 0-919991-48-3.
 The addresses may be somewhat outdated but this is still useful for the guidance on church, especially Roman Catholic, records.

Charlotte Bronte Perry. *The long road, volume 1: The history of the coloured Canadian in Windsor, Ontario, 1867-1967.* Windsor: C.B.Perry, 1967. 211pp., illus. Bibliography.
 A general history of black Canadians in Windsor, with many biographies.

Dora Pineau. *Index for the Essex-Kent counties historical atlas.* Windsor: Essex County branch OGS, 1986. 177pp.
 Every name.

Claudette Piquette Bibeau, Anne-Marie Frenette, Agathe Saumure-Vaillancourt. *Mariages et sépultures, paroisse Notre-Dame-de-Lourdes de Comber, 1948-1987.* Ottawa: Centre franco-ontarienne d'Histoire et de Généalogie, 1990. xiii leaves, 64pp., illus. ISSN: 0823-1575 (Paroisses de l'Ontario français). Index.
    Vol. 21 in the series; names, parents and date.

Claudette Piquette Bibeau et al. *Mariages & sépultures, Saint-Jérôme de Windsor, 1958-1985.* Ottawa: Société franco-ontarienne d'Histoire et de Généalogie, n.d. 72pp., illus. ISBN: 0921448-09-0. Index.
    Vol. 17 in the series "Paroisses de l'Ontario français." Names, parents and date for the marriages; dates of death and burial, parents/spouse, age for the burials.

Claudette Piquette Bibeau et al. *Mariages et sépultures, Sainte-Thérèse de Windsor, 1928-1985.* Ottawa: Société franco-ontarienne d'Histoire et de Généalogie, n.d. 333pp., illus. ISBN: 0921448-10-4. Index.
    Vol. 18 in the series "Paroisses de l'Ontario français." Names, parents, date for the marriages; dates of death and burial, parents/spouse, age for the burials.

Claudette Piquette Bibeau et al. *Mariages, Saint-François-Xavier de Tilbury, 1855-1985.* Ottawa: Société franco-ontarienne d'Histoire et de Généalogie, 1988. 261pp. ISSN: 0823-1575 (Paroisses de l'Ontario français) Index.
    Vol. 16 in the series. Names, parents, date.

Claudette Piquette Bibeau et al. *Mariages, St.-Jean-Baptiste d'Amherstburg, 1802-1985.* Ottawa: Société franco-ontarienne d'Histoire et de Généalogie, 1987. 385pp. ISSN: 0823-1575 (Paroisses de l'Ontario francais). Index.
    Bride, groom, parents, date. Both this volume and the burials (below) are labelled vol. 15 in the series.

Claudette Piquette Bibeau et al. *Sépultures, Saint-François-Xavier de Tilbury, 1855-1985.* Ottawa: Société franco-ontarienne d'Histoire et de Généalogie, 1988. 288pp. ISSN: 0823-1575 (Paroisses de l'Ontario français).
    Vol. 16A in the series. Dates of death and burial, parents/spouse, age.

Claudette Piquette Bibeau et al. *Sépultures, St.-Jean-Baptiste d'Amherstburg, 1802-1985.* Ottawa: Société franco-ontarienne d'Histoire et de Généalogie, 1987. 370pp. ISSN: 0823-1575 (Paroisses de l'Ontario français).
   Name, dates of death and burial, spouse, parents, age.

Register of St. John's church of England at Sandwich in the Western district of the province of Upper Canada, 1802-1827. Windsor: Essex branch OGS/Chatham: Kent branch OGS, 1990. 71pp. Index.
   Records of the earliest Anglican church in this area.

Juliette St-Pierre, Monique Pelland, Marie Cousineau, Charlene Boudreau. *Sépultures, paroisse L'Assomption de Windsor, Ontario, 1768-1985.* Ottawa: Société franco-ontarienne d'Histoire et de Généalogie, 1986. 282pp. ISSN: 0823-1575 (Paroisses de l'Ontario français).
   Vol. 12 in the series. Brief entries in alphabetical order.

Jean Zimmerman. *Index to the 1851 Essex county, Ontario, Canada, census, with a name index to Histoire des Canadiens du Michigan et du comté d'Essex, Ontario.* Lansing: French Canadian Heritage Society of Michigan, 1982. 134pp.
   Alphabetical listing, every name.

Frontenac County

   Cemeteries in Frontenac are published by Kingston branch OGS.

Barbara B. Aitken. *Zion Presbyterian church baptismal roll, 1891-1919; marriage register, 1892-1919.* Kingston: Kingston branch OGS, 1979. 51pp. Index.
   The church is not identified, but may be the current Zion United Church, Kingston.

Barbara B. Aitken & Dawn Broughton. *Tracing your ancestors in Frontenac and Lennox & Addington counties.* Kingston: Kingston branch OGS, 1991. 2d ed. 89pp., illus. ISBN: 1-55034-916-3. Bibliographical references.

Originally published 1987. A handbook, listing repositories, societies, church records in archives, cemeteries, etc. Includes maps of all townships.

Baptisms 1853-1976, Cooke's-Portsmouth United Church, Kingston, Ontario. Kingston: Kingston branch OGS, 1995. viii,121pp. ISBN: 0-77790\-0506-X. Indexed.

The church was originally Presbyterian. The index includes the names of all participants.

Dawn Broughton. *Transcription of Chalmers church registers, baptisms and marriages, 1857-1900.* Kingston: Kingston branch OGS, 1988. 39,36pp. ISBN: 1-55034-031-X. Index.

Full information in computerized format.

Cataraqui Community Cemetery burial register. Kingston: Kingston branch OGS, 1987-1988. 5v. ISBN: 0-920036-99-6 (v.1) Indexes.

Burial records, not stones. Volumes 1-5 cover 1853-1921.

Linda Corupe. *Forty years of Kennebec Twp., Frontenac Co., Ont. (1861-1901).* Bolton: L.Corupe, 1994. 2v. Indexed.

Census transcriptions, civil registration extracts, directories, all indexed.

Linda Corupe. *Index to the 1851 census of Frontenac county, Ontario.* Kingston: Kingston branch OGS, 1989. 79pp. ISBN: 1-55034-378-5.

Although it does not specify, this seems to be a Heads of Families and Strays index.

Margaret M. Coho & Margaret E. Purcell. *Index to volumes 1-6 of Buildings of Architectural and Historic Significance, City of Kingston.* Kingston: Kingston branch OGS, 1995. ISBN: 0-7779-0509-4.

Names of individuals, families, occupations, streets. The original volumes were published by the city, 1971-1985.

Nancy Findlater Cutway. *Burials in St. Paul's (Anglican) churchyard, Kingston, Ontario.* Kingston: Kingston branch OGS, 1992. 18pp., map. ISBN: 1-55075-242-1. Index.

Interment records and an early list of stones.

Cecil F. Deyo, Linda Corupe & R.A. Jones. *Methodist church baptismal records, 1835-1897, Frontenac county, Ontario (excepting Kingston city and township).* Kingston: Kingston branch OGS, 1991. 54pp. ISBN: 1-55034-923-6.

These are the Wesleyan records, full text given.

1844 census of the Catholic population of the mission of Kingston. Kingston: Kingston branch OGS, 1979. 35,7pp. ISBN: 1-55034-012-3. Index.

Typed version of original format. Heads of families, with descriptions of children.

Rose Mary Gibson. *Genealogical sources in the Douglas Library, Kingston, Ont.* Ottawa: Ottawa branch OGS, 1978. 28pp.

The Douglas Library is at Queen's University. This publication is now outdated, but a more current version of this information is available: Barbara B. Aitken's "Genealogical resources at Queen's", *Families*, February 1993 (v.32, no.1).

T.R. Glover & D.D. Calvin. *A corner of empire: the old Ontario strand.* Cambridge, England: Cambridge University Press, 1937. 178pp. Index.

A history of Kingston interwoven with personal commentary, this book may be a painless way to absorb some local history while being entertained.

A. R. Hazelgrove. *Name and place index to Illustrated historical atlas of the counties of Frontenac, Lennox & Addington, Ontario.* Kingston: Hazelgrove, 1973. 59pp.

Edwin E. Horsey. *Kingston a century ago.* Kingston: Kingston Historical Society, 1938. 37pp.

Illustrated historical atlas of Frontenac, Lennox and Addington counties, Ontario. Belleville: Mika, 1972. 105pp., illus. ISBN: 0-919302-14-9.

Originally published by Meacham, Toronto, 1878. Includes maps with names. For *Index*, see Hazelgrove above.

Index to wills probated, Frontenac county, Ontario, Canada, 1858-1973. Kingston: Kingston branch OGS, 1988. 160pp. ISBN: 1-55034-026-3.
> Brief index only. Originals at the Archives of Ontario.

George & Harriett Jeffrey. *Methodist church baptismal records, 1844-1876, city of Kingston and Kingston township, Frontenac county, Ontario.* Kingston: Kingston branch OGS, 1990. 38pp. ISBN: 1-55034-910-4.
> These are the Wesleyan records, full text given.

The Kingston Chronicle. Stratford: Bur-Mor, 1993- (in progress) ISBN: 1-55024-182-6 (v.1) Index.
> Extracts from the newspaper, chiefly births, deaths and marriages, given in full.

Agnes Maule Machar. *The story of Old Kingston.* Toronto: Musson, 1908. 291pp., illus.

Mary Mackie. *First Congregational Church, Kingston, Ontario, marriage register, 1858-1921.* Kingston: Kingston branch OGS, 1992. 17 leaves. ISBN: 1-55075-244-8. Index.
> Full information. SEE ALSO Small below.

Joan Mackinnon. *Kingston cabinetmakers 1800-1867.* Ottawa: National Museums of Canada, 1976. iv,18pp., illus.
> As well as a discussion of their art, a list of the woodworkers themselves is included.

William J. Patterson. *Lilacs and limestone: an illustrated history of Pittsburgh township, 1787-1987.* s.l.: Pittsburgh Historical Society, 1989. 336pp., illus. ISBN: 0-9693944-0-3. Bibliography. Index.

Registers, 1821-1869, St. Andrew's Presbyterian Church, Kingston, Ontario. Kingston: Kingston branch OGS, 1980. various pagings. Indexed.
> Baptisms and marriages, full text.

Registers of St. Patrick's parish, Railton, Ontario, mission to Mill Creek (Odessa), 1844-1875. Kingston: Kingston branch OGS, n.d. 32pp. ISBN: 1-55034-011-5. Indexed.

"Intended to be added to the material called *Kingston, St. Mary's cathedral registers 1816-1869* and *Railton, St. Patrick's parish registers 1844-1872* a copy of which may be seen on microfilm at the Archives of Ontario or the Kingston Public Library."

Bryan Rollason. *County of a thousand lakes: the history of the county of Frontenac, 1673-1973.* Kingston: Frontenac County Council, 1982. 572pp., illus. ISBN: 0-9690461-0-3. Bibliographical references. Index.

St. Andrew's Presbyterian Church, Kingston, Ontario, burial register, 1860-1889. Kingston: Kingston branch OGS, 1993. 22pp. ISBN: 1-55075-254-5. Index.
   Name, age, residence, burial place, interment date; other information if available.

Darrell Small & Nancy Findlater Cutway. *First Congregational Church, Kingston, Ontario, baptismal register, 1849-1920.* Kingston: Kingston branch OGS, 1992. 28pp. ISBN: 1-55075-236-7. Index.
   Name, dates of birth & baptism, parents. SEE ALSO Mackie above.

Larry Turner. *Voyage of a different kind: the Associated Loyalists of Kingston and Adolphustown.* Belleville: Mika, 1984. 180pp., maps. ISBN: 0-919303-81-1. Bibliography. Indexed.
   Brief, readable text which might serve as a useful introduction to Quinte Loyalists, with extensive lists, appendices and bibliographical references.

Russ Waller. *1851 census, Loughborough & Storrington townships, Frontenac County.* Kingston: R.Waller, 1988. various pagings. Index.
   Full transcription with index.

Russ Waller. *1861 census, Frontenac county.* Kingston: R.Waller, 1992-93. 5v., maps. Index.
   Full transcription with index. Volumes for Kingston; Kingston township; Portland; Bedford, Kennebec, Olden, Oso; Portsmouth, the Penitentiary, Rockwood Asylum, Forts Henry & Frederick.

Russ Waller. *Howe Island book of cousins: a marital network file of original settlers of Howe Island, Frontenac county and later generations.* Kingston: Walrus Press, 1987. 81pp.

Russ Waller. *Kingston township, 1851 census.* Kingston: R. Waller, 1988. 114pp. Index.
    Full transcription, with index.

Russ Waller. *Like rabbits in Ernestown!* SEE UNDER Lennox & Addington

Russ Waller. *1901 census, heads & strays index, Frontenac County.* Kingston: R.Waller, 1993. 2v.
    One volume covers Kingston, Portsmouth and the islands, the other the townships.

Russ Waller. *Portland & Hinchinbrooke townships, 1851 census.* Kingston: R.Waller, 1988. 49,11pp. Index.
    Full transcription with index.

Russ Waller. *Wolfe Island, 1851 census.* Kingston: R.Waller, 1988. 62pp. Index.
    Full transcription, with index.

Russ Waller. *Wolfe Island family connections: a marital network file of original settlers and later generations.* Rev.ed. Kingston: R.Waller, 1989. 282pp.
    Originally published 1988.

Loral & Mildred Wanamaker. *Abstracts of surrogate court wills, Kingston and vicinity, 1790-1858.* Kingston: Kingston branch OGS, 1982. 41pp. Indexed.
    Extracted abstracts, originally from the Wanamaker Collection on local families (Kingston branch library, 20 vols.). "The wills...abstracted in this volume pertain to a wider geographical area than modern-day Frontenac County." Originals at the Archives of Ontario.

A.H. Young. *The parish register of Kingston, Upper Canada, 1785-1811.* Kingston: British Whig Publishing, 1921. 207pp., maps. Indexed.

Because of Kingston's physical position (on the way inland) and political importance, the Anglican register of St. George's church is significant.

Glengarry County

Alex W. Fraser. *Gravestones of Glengarry.* Belleville: Mika, 1976-78. 2v., illus. ISBN: 0-919303-08-0 (v.1) Index.
A third volume (ISBN: 0-921307-02-0) was published by Highland Heritage in 1988. The Mika volumes represent a sophisticated departure in cemetery transcription, with commentary on the cemeteries.

Alex W. Fraser. *The Hephzibah church, baptisms, marriages, 1899-1911 and name index (Williamstown, Ontario).* Lancaster: Highland Heritage, 1986. 91pp. ISBN: 0-9692172-8-5.
Full entries, but no index.

Alex W. Fraser. *The Methodist church, baptisms, marriages, 1878-1903, and name index (Lancaster, Ontario).* Lancaster: Highland Heritage, 1986. 96pp. ISBN: 0-9692172-9-3. Index.
Full entries, including indications of blank spaces in the registers.

Alex W. Fraser. *St. Andrew's Presbyterian church, Martintown, Ontario, baptisms, marriages & deaths, 1925-1990.* Lancaster: Highland Heritage, 1992. 323pp. ISBN: 0-921307-34-9. Index.
The church records are augmented by comments. The introduction explains the interrelations between these church records and others in the area.

Alex W. Fraser. *St. Finnan's church records, name index, 1836-1883 (Alexandria, Ontario)* Lancaster: Highland Heritage, 1986. 3v. ISBN: 0-9692172-5-0 (v.1).
Full entries.

The Glengarrian. Stratford: Bur-Mor, 1990- . v.1- (August 1895-) ISBN: 1-55-24-093-5 (v.1). Indexed.
Another in W. Craig Burtch's series of extractions from 19th century Ontario newspapers. *The Glengarrian* was published in Alexandria. Burtch has extracted birth, death and marriage notices in

their entirety. The notices tend to be longer than usual in other papers, especially the marriages, which provide interesting details.

John Graham Harkness. *Stormont, Dundas and Glengarry...* SEE UNDER Stormont County.

Hubert Houle. ***Répertoire des mariages du comté de Glengarry, Ontario.*** Ottawa: Centre de généalogie S.C., 1983. 2 v. Index.
Marriages performed at 16 Roman Catholic churches in 14 communities in the county, beginning in 1802.

Illustrated historical atlas... SEE UNDER Dundas County

Duncan W. MacDonald. ***Lochiel 1820-1884 parish register.*** s.l.: Leeds-Grenville branch OGS, n.d. 186pp. ISBN: 0-921133-02-2. Index.
Records of St. Columba's Presbyterian Church, Lochiel. Baptisms & marriages.

Duncan W. MacDonald. ***The parish registers of St. Raphael's, Glengarry, Ontario.*** s.l.: D.MacDonald, 1988. 3 v.., maps. ISBN: 0-921133-08-1 (Deaths 1804-1856). Index.
Deaths 1804-1856; baptisms 1804-1822/marriages 1804-7, 1815-22; births/marriages 1823-31. Full details.

Royce MacGillivray & Ewan Ross. ***A history of Glengarry.*** Belleville: Mika, 1979. 709pp. ISBN: 0-929303-32-3. Bibliography. Index.

Clive Marin. *Stormont, Dundas and Glengarry...* SEE UNDER Dundas County

Grenville County see Leeds-Grenville

Grey County
Cemeteries in Grey are published by Bruce-Grey branch OGS.

Melba Morris Croft. ***City of Owen Sound, 1921.*** Owen Sound: M.Croft, 1990. 152pp., illus. ISBN: 0-9690315-7-2. Indexed.
Continues: *Growth of a county town.* This is the cover title; the caption title is: *History of Owen Sound 1921.* More history and social

background for the city, using the newspaper as the source. Its sequel is: *Renewal of a Canadian port*.

Melba Morris Croft. ***Growth of a county town: Owen Sound 1900-1920.*** Owen Sound: M.Croft, 1984. xvi,348pp., illus. ISBN: 0-9690315-4-8. Indexed.
    Using material from the Owen Sound *Advertiser* as her base, Croft describes life in Owen Sound, at the same time both writing a history and journeying through the backwaters of social life. This provides a cornucopia of material for family historians. *City of Owen Sound 1921* continues the story.

Melba Morris Croft. ***Lest we forget.*** Owen Sound: M.Croft, 1981. 24 leaves, illus.
    Lists of those who fought and died in World War I, particularly those who served with the 147th Battalion. Although Croft says the list consists of those "living at Owen Sound", the number might suggest others from Grey and surrounding counties are also included. Also a short history of the Grey Regiment, useful for adding colour to family histories.

Melba Morris Croft. ***Renewal of a Canadian port: (Owen Sound on Georgian Bay).*** Owen Sound: M.Croft, 1993. ii,371pp., illus. ISBN: 0-9690315-8-0. Indexed.
    Continuing her year-by-year examination of the city's history through its newspaper columns, Croft covers the early and mid-1920s. Sequel to: *City of Owen Sound 1921*.

T Arthur Davidson. ***A new history of the county of Grey and the many communities within its boundaries and the city of Owen Sound.*** Owen Sound: Grey County Historical Society, 1972. 433pp., illus.

First Methodist Church, Owen Sound, marriage records. Owen Sound: Bruce & Grey branch OGS, n.d. (in progress)
    Only one volume published, with marriages from 1895 to 1901.

Katie Harrison. ***Priceville and its roots (routes).*** Priceville: Priceville (and area) Historical Society, 1992. 276pp., illus. ISBN: 0-9696807-0-8. Index.

A history of the town of Durham, 1842-1994. Durham: Durham Historical Committee, 1994. 290pp., illus. ISBN: 0-9699201-0-5. Index.

Illustrated historical atlas... SEE UNDER Bruce County

Jopie Loughead & Alfreda Veenstra. *Meaford & Collingwood papers: index to births, marriages & deaths.* Owen Sound: Bruce & Grey branch OGS, 1993. 2 v. ISBN: 1-55132-322-2 (v.1) Indexes.
Volume 1 covers 1869-1900; v.2, 1901-1910. Includes material from a variety of newspapers.

E.L. Marsh. *A history of the county of Grey.* Owen Sound: Fleming Publishing, 1931. 487pp., illus.
Extensive history, including a full reproduction of the name lists from the 1865 directory of the county.

Reminiscences of north Sydenham: a retrospective sketch of the villages of Leith and Annan, Grey county, Ontario. Owen Sound: Richardson, Bond & Wright, 1924. 256pp.
Similar to others of its era, it is more personal than community history, but from a day when everyone knew everyone. Many names.

Betty Warrilow. *Tracing your ancestors in Bruce & Grey.* SEE UNDER Bruce County

Haldimand County

Cemeteries in Haldimand are published by Haldimand County branch OGS.

Shirley Dosser. *Nanticoke through the years.* Simcoe: Norfolk Historical Society, 1990. 146pp., illus.
A village history, including the surrounding area.

Farmers' directory for the county of Haldimand 1891: Canboro', Cayuga, Dunn, Moulton, Oneida townships. Brantford: Brant County branch OGS, n.d. 40pp.
Photocopies of pages from an earlier directory. In a separate publication: Rainham, Seneca, Sherbrooke, Walpole townships.

The Grand River Sachem. Stratford: Bur-Mor, 1986. 19pp. ISBN: 1-55024-033-1. Index.

This newspaper was published in Caledonia. Craig Burtch has extracted chiefly births, deaths and marriages for the period 1866-1868, texts given in full.

Illustrated historical atlas of the counties of Haldimand and Norfolk. s.l.: s.n., n.d. 111pp., illus.

Originally published separately by Page, Toronto, in 1877 and 1879. Reprinted in this edition in the 1970s. Includes maps with names.

The Jarvis Record. Stratford: Bur-Mor, 1994- . (in progress) ISBN: 1-55024-188-5 (v.1) Index.

Extracts from the newspaper, chiefly births, deaths and marriages, given in full. Volumes 1-4 cover 1882 to 1911.

Cheryl MacDonald. *Heritage highlights; stories from Haldimand and Norfolk.* Nanticoke: Heronwood Writing Services, 1994. 120pp. Bibliography. Index.

A collection of newspaper columns from the *Simcoe & Nanticoke Times.*

Marriage records 1838-1870 of the Rev. Bold Cudmore Hill M.A. S.P.G. missionary at York, Grand River, Canada West. Hamilton: Hamilton branch OGS, 1979? 23, xii pp. Index.

From an original register at McMaster University library.

Barbara Martindale. *Caledonia along the Grand River.* Toronto: Natural History/Natural Heritage, 1995. 127pp., illus. ISBN: 0-920474-81-0. Indexed.

A brief history of the town.

Robert Bertram Nelles. *County of Haldimand in the days of Auld Lang Syne.* Port Hope: Hamly Press, 1905. 117pp. Indexed.

Chatty reminiscences with many names.

William John Quinsey. *York, Grand River, its early history and directory, 1834-1860.* York: York, Grand River, Historical Society, 1991. 290pp., illus.

The 'directory' is actually a biographical dictionary of settlers in the area, very useful.

Lorne Sorge. *Canborough: come with us on a journey through historic Canborough.* s.l.: Canborough Township Historical Committee, 1991. 96pp., illus. ISBN: 0-9695622-0-9.

Corlene Taylor & Gregory Miller. *1828 census returns, Haldimand county.* St. Catharines: Niagara Peninsula branch, OGS, 1992. rev. 6pp. ISBN: 0-9200036-59-7. Indexed.
Originally published 1985, revised 1986, revised again 1992. Complete transcription, including Rainham township.

Corlene Taylor & Gregory Miller. *Haldimand county collector's roll, 1837.* St. Catharines: Niagara Peninsula branch OGS, 1986. Revised ed. 5pp. Index.
Tax records.

William Yeager. *Haldimand county marriages, 1803-1856.* Simcoe: Norfolk Historical Society, 1983. 80pp.
Full text, from a variety of sources.

Haliburton County

Cemeteries in Haliburton are published by Kawartha branch OGS and the Haliburton Highlands Genealogical Group.

Leopolda z. L. Dobrzensky. *They worked and prayed together: Italians in Haliburton county.* Haliburton: L.Dobrzensky, 1988. 55pp., illus.

History of Haliburton county... SEE UNDER Peterborough County, the listing for *History of the county of Peterborough....*

Nila Reynolds. *In quest of yesterday.* Minden: Provisional County of Haliburton, 1973. 3d ed. 356pp., illus. Index.
First & 2d eds. 1968. A history of the county, including community histories.

Halton County

Cemeteries in Halton are published by Halton-Peel branch OGS.

Margaret Beettam. ***Brampton, the Conservator, an index.*** Oakville: Halton-Peel branch OGS, 1989- (in progress) ISBN: 0-9693991-0-3 (v.1).
Name and date, newspaper page. Volumes 1-7 cover 1876 to 1919.

Margaret Beettam. ***The Brampton Times, an index 1867-1871 (not complete) plus April 19, 1872 and July 17, 1874.*** Oakville: Halton-Peel branch OGS, 1990. 43 leaves. ISBN: 0-9693991-3-8.
Name, date, newspaper page.

J. Eric Blaney & Alex S. Cooke. ***Halton marriage register 1870-1873.*** Oakville: Halton-Peel branch OGS, 1993. Rev. ed. 82pp. Index.
Full transcriptions of the registrations in Halton district, with surname index.

The Brampton Times. Stratford: Bur-Mor, 1993- . (in progress) ISBN: 1-55024-158-3 (v.1). Index.
Another in the series of full extractions, with index, mainly of BDMs. Volumes 1-2 cover June 1867 to July 1874.

Brampton's 100th anniversary. Brampton: City of Brampton, 1973. 164, 110pp., illus.

Alex S. Cooke. ***A list of birth, marriages and deaths in the Halton journal, 1855-1858.*** Oakville: Halton-Peel branch OGS, 1990. 13pp. Indexes.
Full text and indexes.

Halton-Peel marriages performed at St. Andrew's Presbyterian Church, Toronto, 1832-1868. Oakville: Halton-Peel branch OGS, n.d. 13pp.
Full details.

Illustrated historical atlas of the county of Halton, Ont. Port Elgin: Cumming, 1971. 72pp., illus.

Originally published by Walker & Miles, Toronto, 1877. Includes maps with names.

Mary Jones & Trudy Mann. ***Halton-Peel marriages performed at St. James Anglican Cathedral, Toronto, 1800-1896.*** Oakville: Halton-Peel branch OGS, n.d. unpaged.
       Full details. Taken from J.R. Robertson's *Landmarks of Toronto.*

Marriage register of Elder Hugh Reid... SEE UNDER Wellington County

J.M.B. Rowe. ***Bicentennial directory of Glen Williams.*** s.l.: s.n., 1984. 35pp.
       Includes 1933 voters' list.

J.M.B. Rowe. ***Collections.*** Georgetown: Esquesing Historical Society, 1990-1995. 3 v. ISBN: 0-921901-10-0 (v.3)
       The Esquesing Historical Society has published three volumes of miscellaneous history essays. The first is called *Archival papers* and the latter two *Collections.* The essays are varied and worth investigating.

J.M.B. Rowe. ***Glen Williams on the Credit River.*** Georgetown: Esquesing Historical Society, 1993. 53pp., illus. ISBN: 0-921901-18-6.
       Village history.

Rural mail directory Halton county and district, December 1925. Georgetown: Esquesing Historical Society, 1990. 48pp. ISBN: 0-921901-11-9.
       Includes parts of Peel and Wellington.

Jan Speers and Ruth Holt. ***Research in Halton and Peel: a genealogical handbook.*** Agincourt: Generation Press, 1980. 38pp., maps. ISBN: 0-920830-18-8.
       Now somewhat outdated, but worth examining as a pointer to timeless resources.

Voters lists for 1875, municipality of the township of Esquesing.
Georgetown: Esquesing Historical Society, 1992. unpaged. ISBN: 0-921901-15-1.
    Reproduction of the original list.

Margaret Williams & Jan Speers. *People of Halton: indexes to genealogical sources in Halton.* Oakville: M. Williams, 1983. 96pp. Bibliography.
    Indexes to a random assortment of genealogical resources.

Hastings County
Cemeteries in Hastings are published by Quinte branch OGS and Susan Bergeron.

Susan Bergeron. *Sidney township census 1881.* Brighton: S.Bergeron, 1993. 57 leaves. Index.
    Every name but not full details. The same author/publisher has produced Sidney census books for 1851, 1861, 1871, 1891.

Susan Bergeron. *Trenton census, 1891, Hastings county, Ontario.* Brighton: S.Bergeron, 1992. 59 leaves. Index.
    Every name but not full details. The same author/publisher has produced Trenton census books for 1871, 1881.

Gerald E. Boyce. *Eldorado: Ontario's first gold rush.* Toronto: Natural Heritage/Natural History, 1992. 160pp., illus. ISBN: 0-920474-74-8. Bibliography. Index.
    Eldorado is north of Madoc.

Gerald E. Boyce. *Historic Hastings.* Belleville: Hastings County Council, 1967. 385pp., illus. Indexed.

Gerald E. Boyce et al. *Sidney township 200, 1790-1990.* Belleville: Hastings County Historical Society, 1990. 78pp., illus.
    Year-by-year history of township government.

Patricia Cole & Hilda Manning. *Methodist church baptismal records, 1840-1887, Sidney township and Tyendinaga township, Hastings county, Ontario.* Kingston: Kingston branch OGS, 1990. 50pp. ISBN: 1-55034-908-2. Index.

These are the Wesleyan records, with full text given, in the order registered.

1860-61 directory of the county of Hastings. Belleville: Mackenzie Bowell/Intelligencer, 1860. 326pp., maps.

Allan R.D. Hazelgrove. *Name and place index to Illustrated historical atlas of the counties of Hastings and Prince Edward.* Kingston: Brown & Martin, 1974.

Illustrated historical atlas of Hastings and Prince Edward counties, Ontario. Belleville: Mika, 1972. 83pp. ISBN: 0-919302-15-7.

Originally published by Belden, Toronto, 1878. Includes maps with names. For *Index*, see Hazelgrove above.

Madawaska Valley District High School. *The 1881 census of Hastings county: Bangor township and Wicklow and McClure townships.* Ottawa: Ottawa branch OGS, 1990. 30pp. ISBN: 1-55034-893-0.

Full text with index.

Allen D. Piper. *Marriages from the Hungerford township registers, Hastings county, Province of Ontario.* s.l.: s.n., 1976. 75pp.

Covers fifty years, 1876-1926. Full entries including clergyman under the groom's name, index for brides.

Ruth Tierney. *Echoes from the past in Hastings county and vicinity.* Belleville: Mika, 1986. 158pp., illus. 0-921341-04-0.

Elizabeth Wood. *Methodist church baptismal records, 1843-1876, Madoc township, Hastings county, Ontario.* Kingston: Kingston branch OGS, 1990. unpaged. ISBN: 1-55034-377-7.

These are the Wesleyan records, with full text given.

Huron County

Cemeteries in Huron are published by Huron County branch OGS.

The Clinton New Era. Stratford: Bur-Mor, 1994- . (in progress) ISBN: 1-55024-200-8. Index.
   Extracts from the newspaper, chiefly births, deaths and marriages, given in full. Volumes 1-4 cover 1874-1878.

Walter E. Creery. *Between the fences: Usborne township, 1842-1992.* Exeter: Usborne Township Council, 1991. 597pp., illus.
   Includes many family histories.

Early Wesleyan Methodist baptismal register extractions for Huron county. Goderich: Huron County branch OGS, 1993. 4 v. ISBN: 1-55116-798-0 (v.1)
   v.1: Hullett, McKillop, Morris; v.2: Hay, Stanley, Stephen, Tuckersmith, Usborne; v.3: Grey, Howick, Turnberry; v.4: Ashfield, Colborne, Goderich, Wawanosh. Full text.

John Elder. *Tuckersmith pioneers, being a series of articles about early settlers written by Mr. John Elder for the Huron Expositor, Seaforth.* Goderich: Huron County branch OGS, 1992. 48pp. ISBN: 1-55116-796-4.
   Colourful anecdotes in an old-fashioned style.

William Sherwood Fox. *'T aint runnin' no more; the story of Grand Bend, the Pinery and the old river bed.* London: Wendell Holmes, 1946. 55pp.

Gavin Hamilton Green. *The old log school and Huron old boys in pioneer days.* Goderich: Signal-Star, 1939. 217pp., illus.
   School experiences and interesting characters he knew: Dungannon, Port Albert, Goderich, Tiverton and Sheppardton.

Illustrated historical atlas of Huron county, Ontario. Belleville: Mika, 1972. xxiv,76pp., illus. ISBN: 0-919302-22-X.
   Originally published by Belden, Toronto, 1879. Includes maps with names.

Alison Lobb. *Goderich township families 1985.* Clinton: A. Lobb, 1986. 830pp., illus. ISBN: 0-9692322-0-9.

Entirely genealogies, supplied by the families themselves. Companion to *The township of Goderich history* (1985) from the same author.

1984 Huron county historical atlas. Goderich: County of Huron, 1984. 350pp., illus. ISBN: 0-96992120-0-3. Index.

Brief histories, biographies, places and maps.

James Scott. *The settlement of Huron county.* Toronto: Ryerson, 1966. xiii,328pp. Indexed.

A very readable account, also useful to those with interests in surrounding counties. The stories it provides might be useful for colour in family histories.

Kenora District

Cemeteries in Kenora are available from Nor-West Genealogical and Historical Society. SEE ALSO Note under Rainy River District.

Evergreen reflections. Vermilion Bay: Nor-West Historical Society, 1986. 478pp., illus. ISBN: 0-88925-528-8. Bibliography. Index.

Local tales, with many family histories, of the Vermilion Bay area, including Blue Lake, Machin, Minnitaki, Pine Grove, Waldhof.

G. Earl McNicholl. *Ingolf.* s.l.: s.n., n.d. 400pp., illus. Index.

An anecdotal history of the Ingolf area, largely consisting of family accounts of specific activities and places. The volume was published about 1995. Another volume of further reminiscence is due in 1997.

Kent County

Cemeteries in Kent are published by Kent County branch OGS.

Wendy Lee Barry. *Harwich township and vicinity marriages, 1870-1876.* s.l: s.n.,n.d. unpaged.

From material located by chance in the township office, now owned by the Kent County branch OGS. Full transcriptions, listed under groom's name, with brides index. These may or may not be included in the civil registration records now available through the Archives of Ontario.

Wendy Lee Barry. *Harwich Twp. assessment rolls, Kent county, 1855.* Chatham: Kent County branch OGS, 1986. unpaged.
 An attempt to replace the missing 1851 census for Harwich. Name, age, address.

Wendy Lee Barry. *Raleigh township statute labour, 1838-1847.* s.l.: s.n., 1985. unpaged.
 "The assessment act stated that every male between the ages of 16 and 60 had to put in a minimum two days statute labour." This is a list of names, with year-by-year accounting of days worked. The original lists are at the Chatham-Kent Museum.

Wendy Lee Barry. *United Presbyterian church of Blenheim & Harwich, baptisms, 1855-1887.* Chatham: Kent County branch OGS, n.d. unpaged. ISBN: 1-551156-291-1. Index.
 Full text.

Helen A. Blackburn & Judith A. Mitton. *Crown land first patentees, Kent county, Ontario.* Chatham: Kent County branch OGS, 1985. unpaged, maps.
 "...answers two questions: where did my ancestor settle, and when did he obtain his land." *Index* by Peggy Stenton published separately.

Helen A. Blackburn & Judith Mitton. *Kent county death census 1871.* Chatham: Kent County branch OGS, n.d. unpaged.
 The mortality schedules were missing from the original filming of the census. This transcribed that material. Now also accessible through the 1871 census index (SEE Elliott, B. in the general section). Full text.

Blenheim Methodist church marriage register, Aug. 1896-Sep. 1923. Chatham: Kent County branch OGS, n.d. 27pp. ISBN: 1-55116-293-8.
 Full text, no index.

Robert Brandon. *A history of Dresden.* Dresden: Dresden times, 1954. 64pp., illus.

Nancy Cameron. ***Locke & Co. funeral home records, Ridgetown, Ontario, 1882-1950.*** Chatham: Kent County branch OGS, 1994. 2 v. ISBN: 1-55116-330-6. Index.
   Full text. This title was withdrawn from sale soon after publication and cannot easily be located.

The Chatham Gleaner of News, literature and general intelligence, 1844-1849. Stratford: Bur-Mor, 1988. 20pp. ISBN: 1-55024-059-5. Index.
   Extracts from the newspaper, chiefly births, deaths and marriages, text given in full.

The Chatham papers: a composite. Stratford: Bur-Mor, 1988-92. 2 v. ISBN: 1-55024-058-7 (v.1). Index.
   Extracts from a variety of Chatham newspapers, chiefly births, deaths and marriages, text given in full. The two volumes include material from 1848 to 1883.

Lynn & Helen Clark. ***Lost in Middlesex county: Kent county names extracted from the Middlesex Co. marriage register, 1849-1869.*** Chatham: Kent County branch OGS, 1989. 12,5pp.
   Full text.

Donna J. Cofell. ***Population return for the township of Howard for 1846.*** Chatham: Kent County branch OGS, 1992. 10pp. ISBN: 1-55116-289-X.
   Heads of families, with numbers of family members and religion.

Commemorative biographical record of the county of Kent, Ontario. Toronto: Beers, 1904.
   Index by Helen Blackburn & Dahn D. Higley published by Kent County branch OGS 1989.

Linda Corupe. ***Wesleyan Methodist baptismal register...*** Bolton: L. Corupe. (in progress) Indexed.
   Brief publications extracting Wesleyan baptisms from the central registers at the United Church Archives. Townships already published: Chatham, Harwich, Camden West, Howard.

Joan Abele Griffin. ***Raleigh twp. collectors rolls, Kent county, 1852.*** s.l.: s.n., n.d. unpaged.
> Name, lot and concession only. Original rolls at Chatham Public Library.

Illustrated historical atlas... SEE UNDER Essex County

The Kent Advertiser: commercial, agricultural and political journal, 1850-1855. Stratford: Bur-Mor, n.d. 6pp. ISBN: 1-55024-061-7. Index.
> Extracts from the newspaper, published in Chatham, chiefly births, deaths and marriages, texts given in full.

Kent county census, 1861. Chatham: Kent County branch OGS, 1987-1991. 10 v.
> Full text.

Kent county marriages, 1857-1869. Chatham: Kent County branch OGS, 1993. 2 v. ISBN: 1-55116-309-8.
> Includes 1858-69 ledgers from the Archives of Ontario plus much supplemental information, including marriages known to be missing from the ledgers.

Kentiana: the story of the settlement and development of the county of Kent summarized from the records of the Kent Historical Society. Chatham?: Kent Historical Society, 1939. 105,xpp. Index.
> A collection of essays.

Ruth L. McMahon. ***Dresden Presbyterian Church, Kent county, Ontario, baptisms, 1881-1908.*** Chatham: Kent County branch OGS, 1989. 10pp.
> Name, dates of birth & baptism, father's name only (mother's name not included). "Not intended to be a transcription."

Ruth L. McMahon. ***Wallaceburg Presbyterian Church, Kent county, Ontario, baptisms, 1882-1902, marriages, 1896-1905.*** Chatham: Kent County branch OGS, 1989. 1 v. (various pagings). Index.
> Brief entries only, computerized format.

Leslie Mancell. *Chatham Primitive Methodist Church, marriages, 1860-1883, an index of names.* Chatham?: Kent County branch OGS?, 1986. unpaged.
>Index to extractions at the Chatham Public Library.

Leslie Mancell. *A guide to some Presbyterian church marriages 1896-1900, baptisms 1866-1901; Botany, Thamesville & Reserve congregations of the Presbyterian church.* Chatham: Kent County branch OGS, 1989. 9pp.
>Computerized index only.

Judith A. Mitton. *Census, Kent county, 1851.* Chatham: Kent County branch OGS, 1986. 5 v. Indexes.
>Full text. Includes part of the county only: town & township of Chatham, Howard, Orford, agricultural.

Judith A. Mitton & Joan Abele Griffin. *Index to Kent county, Ontario, marriage registers, 1857-1869.* Chatham?: Kent county branch OGS?, 1985. unpaged.
>Other counties in Ontario have 1858-1869 marriage indexes published by Generation Press, but Kent's was produced first, and locally. 4600 entries; index only (full transcription must be obtained from the microfilm).

Janet Nelson. *Wayne county marriages: people from Kent county, Ontario, who were married in Wayne county, Michigan, 1839-1869.* Chatham: Kent County branch OGS, n.d. 19 leaves. ISBN: 1-55116-322-5. Index.

Claudette Piquette Bibeau et al. *Mariages et sépultures, paroisse l'Immaculée-Conception de Paincourt, 1851-1988.* Ottawa: Centre franco-ontarienne d'Histoire et de Généalogie, 1990. xviii,252pp., illus. ISSN: 0823-1575 (Paroisses de l'Ontario français). Index.
>Vol. 20 in the series. Name, parents, date.

Claudette Piquette Bibeau et al. *Mariages et sépultures, St.-Philippe, Grande-Pointe, Ontario, 1886-1992.* Ottawa: Société franco-ontarienne d'Histoire et de Généalogie, 1992. xi,256pp., illus. ISSN: 0823-1575 (Paroisses de l'Ontario français). Index.

Vol. 26 in the series. Names, parents, dates. The town is known in English as Big Point.

Arlie C. Robbins. *Legacy to Buxton.* Merlin: A.C.Robbins, 1983. 261pp., illus.
History of the black settlement of Kent county, focusing on Raleigh township. Many names and pictures.

Tracing your family in Kent county. Chatham: Kent County branch OGS, 1988. Updated. 60pp.
Originally published 1979.

United Presbyterian church of Blenheim & Harwich, marriages, 1854-1894. Chatham: Kent County branch OGS, 1993. 54pp. ISBN: 1-555116-311-X. Index.
Full information in computerized format.

West Kent militia, 2nd Kent militia, St. Clair volunteers, pay list, 1838. Sarnia: Lambton County branch OGS, 1989. 19pp. ISBN: 1-55034-998-8.
Includes facsimile signatures of soldiers. "men for these units were mainly from...Euphemia and Dawn...Camden and Zone."

Marilyn E. Wild. *Early Chatham Presbyterian marriages, 1848-1869.* Chatham: Kent County branch OGS, 1987. unpaged.
The original can be seen at the Presbyterian Church in Canada Archives, Toronto or on microfilm through the LDS Family History Library.

Lambton County

Cemeteries in Lambton are published by Lambton County branch OGS.

Belden's Illustrated historical atlas of the county of Lambton, Ontario, 1880. Sarnia: Edward Phelps, 1973. 80pp., illus.
Includes maps with names.

Sara Leitch Campbell. *Brooke township history, 1833-1933.* Sarnia: Lambton County branch OGS, 1995. 171,23pp., illus. ISBN: 0-7779-0011-4. Index.

Originally compiled by the Brooke Women's Institute and published 1936 without the index.

Donald W. Carpenter. *Sombra township 1861 census.* Corunna: Past to Present, n.d. 57pp. ISBN: 0-9695558-7-3.
Transcription plus index.

Donald W. Carpenter. *Sombra township 1881 census, including Walpole Island.* Corunna: Past to Present, n.d. 116,24,14pp. ISBN: 0-9695558-3-0.
Transcription plus index.

Beatrice L. Clark. *Thedford centennial, 1877-1977.* s.l.: s.n., 1977. 124pp., illus.

Commemorative biographical record of the county of Lambton, Ontario. Toronto: Beers, 1906. 840pp., ports. Index.
Extensive biographies. A more complete *Index* is published by Lambton County branch OGS (1989; ISBN: 1-55034-556-7).

Community of Lambton gazetteer, commercial advertiser and business directory, 1864-5. Sarnia: Lambton County branch OGS, n.d. unpaged.
Reprint, originally published in Sarnia in 1864.

Jean Turnbull Elford. *Canada West's last frontier: a history of Lambton.* Sarnia: Lambton County Historical Society, 1982. 189pp., illus. Index.
Includes community histories.

John A. Huey. *The wardens, councillors, parliamentary representatives, judicial officers and county officials of the county of Lambton for 100 years from 1849 to 1949.* Sarnia: Lambton County Council, 1949. 111pp., ports.
Lists of names, some with brief biographies and portraits.

William Frederick Johnson. *More of Arkona through the years, concluding in 1988.* Forest: J.B.Pole Printing, 1988. 77pp., illus.

A.J. Johnston. *Lambton county names and places.* s.l.: Lambton County Council, 1925. 55pp., illus.

Geographical name history, with many personal names.

Lambton county assessment rolls: 1851 Bosanquet township, 1852 Enniskillen township. Sarnia: Lambton County branch OGS, 1993. 12pp. ISBN: 0-7779-0010-6.

These townships are missing for the 1851 census and this is meant as a substitute.

Lambton county census, 1881. Sarnia: Lambton County branch OGS, 1989-1990. 12 v.

Heads of families and strays index. For Sombra section, see Donald Carpenter (above).

Lambton county marriages from early Middlesex marriage register, 1848-1869. Sarnia: Lambton County branch OGS, 1989. 29, 12pp. ISBN: 2-55034-558-3. Index.

From a Middlesex county register filmed for the LDS Family History Library.

Lambton county owner/occupancy index of rural township lots, 1924. Sarnia: Lambton County branch OGS, 1985. various pagings, maps.

The equivalent of a rural directory for 1924.

Lambton ministers' records. Sarnia: Lambton County branch OGS, 1989- . (in progress) ISBN: 1-55034-553-2 (v.1) Index.

Collected, transcribed registers which may be too slight to be published separately. The first volume contains three registers, all Methodist; v.2 contains churches in Forest.

Lambton settlers series. Sarnia: Lambton County branch OGS, n.d. (in progress) Indexes.

Collections of family history essays by various authors. As of 1995, three volumes had been published: *Early days along the St. Clair* (Mugan, Sutherland, Talfourd, Warwick, Johnston); *More early days along the St. Clair* (Bury, McDonald, Vidal, Flintoft); *Early days in Brooke & Warwick* (many families).

Victor Lauriston. *Lambton's hundred years, 1849-1949.* Sarnia: Haines Frontier Printing, 1949. 335p.
  Early history, largely political. *Index* by G.L. Smith published by Lambton County Library in 1971.

D.F. McWatt, John A. Huey, John A. Hair. *History of Lambton county officials, 125 years, 1850-1975.* Sarnia: Haines, 1975? 126pp., ports.
  Lists, and brief biographies of officials.

Minishenhying Anishnaabe-aki: Walpole Island, the soul of Indian territory. Wallaceburg: Nin-da-waab-jig, 1989. 129pp. ISBN: 0-921186-06-1. Bibliography.
  History, principally of the 19th century, of the island.

Eleanor Nielsen. *The Forest Free Press index of births, deaths, marriages.* Forest: E.Nielsen, 1984-86. 2 v.
  v.1, 1898-1907; v.2, 1908-1923. Principal details only.

Eleanor Nielsen. *Index of marriages of Plympton township residents, 1833-1869.* Forest: E. Nielsen, 1983. unpaged.
  From "widely scattered sources", either church registers or newspaper accounts.

Eleanor Nielsen. *Lambton county marriage register, 1858-1869, Index.* Sarnia: Lambton County branch OGS, 1989. 67pp. ISBN: 1-55034-552-4.
  Couples' names and date only. Original ledgers at the Archives of Ontario.

Eleanor Nielsen. *Lambton resources for family history research.* Sarnia: Lambton County branch OGS, 1993. Revised. 32pp. ISBN: 1-55034-901-5.
  Originally published 1989. A brief guide, but contains many addresses.

Eleanor Nielsen. *Plympton township vital statistics 1870.* Sarnia: Lambton County branch OGS, n.d. 12pp. ISBN: 1-55034-555-9.
  From an original township record book at the University of Western Ontario.

Eleanor Nielsen. *Plympton township's rural cemeteries.* Forest: E. Nielsen, 1980. 97pp. Index.
Transcriptions which predate OGS work in this area, but of OGS standard.

Eleanor Nielsen. *The Sarnia militia pay lists 1838.* Sarnia: Lambton County branch OGS, 1992. 17pp. ISBN: 1-555075-200-6.
Includes facsimile signatures of soldiers. Lambton County branch has also published a Warwick list, 1838 (1989) and a Plympton list, 1838 (1992). For a Kent list which includes parts of modern-day Lambton, see under Kent County.

The Sarnia observer. Stratford: Bur-Mor, 1992-   . (in progress) ISBN: 1-55024-126-5 (v.1) Indexes.
Full texts of newspaper items, mostly BDMs. The first volume in the series has a more complex title reflecting the early history of the paper. Volumes 1-13 cover 1853-1878.

Western district, 1842-1849, Lambton county, census, assessments, township elections, teachers. Sarnia: Lambton County branch OGS, 1994. 38pp. ISBN: 0-7779-0020-3.

Lanark County

Cemeteries for Lanark county are published by Leeds-Grenville branch and Ottawa branch OGS, and the Lanark County Genealogical Society.

Peter Andersen & Hubert Houle. *Mariages catholiques de la région de Perth, Ontario.* Ottawa: Centre de généalogie S.C., 1986. 202pp. ISBN: 0-88662-106-2. Index.
Includes Carleton Place, Ferguson's Falls, Merrickville, Perth, Smith's Falls, Stanleyville, Westport.

Peter Anderson & Hubert Houle. *Mariages protestants de la région de Perth, Ontario.* Ottawa: Centre de généalogie S.C., 1986. 203pp. ISBN: 0-88662-104-6. Index.
Marriages from 18 churches, mostly from villages in Lanark, mostly Presbyterian.

The Bathurst Courier. Stratford: Bur-Mor, 1988-1992. 7 v.
ISBN: 1-55-24-076-5 (v.1.) Indexed.
    Part of W. Craig Burtch's series of abstracts from 19th century Ontario newspapers. *The Bathurst Courier,* published in Perth, underwent a number of name changes, eventually becoming *The Perth Courier.* These volumes extract birth, death and marriage announcements, and occasional other news items, given in their entirety. Vols. 1-7 cover August 1834-December 1858.

Carol Bennett. *The Lanark Society settlers.* Renfrew: Juniper Books, 1991. 232pp. ISBN: 0-919137-24-5. Index.
    Early settlers in Lanark, many from Lanarkshire, Scotland but others from Ireland. An alphabetical view of early families.

Ruth G. Burritt. *Burritt's Rapids, 1793-1900.* Thornbury: Conestoga Press, 1993. 63pp., illus. ISBN: 0-919615-26-0. Bibliography. Index.

The history of Smiths Falls. Smiths Falls: Smiths Falls Historical Society, n.d. 1 v. (unpaged), illus.

Alice M. Hughes. *Index to the 1851 census of Canada West, Lanark county, Montague township.* Ottawa: Ottawa branch OGS, 1990. 12pp.
    There are similar indexes for Montague to the 1861 and 1881 census, also by Hughes.

Alice M. Hughes. *Index to the 1891 census of Ontario, Lanark County.* Ottawa: Ottawa branch OGS, 1991. 55pp. ISBN: 1-55075-064-6.
    Heads of families and strays index.

Illustrated historical atlas of Lanark county, 1880; illustrated historical atlas of Renfrew county, 1881, H. Beldon [sic] & Co., Toronto; map of the counties of Lanark and Renfrew from actual surveys under the direction of H.F. Walling...1863. Port Elgin: Cumming, 1972. 68pp., illus.
    The atlases were originally published separately and include maps with names. The 1863 map was a wall hanging, here broken into pieces; the names are difficult to read.

Mildred R. Livingston. *The 1817 census of Perth, Lanark county, Ontario.* Prescott: Livingston, n.d. 9pp. ISBN: 0-920992-05-6.
Names only, but full lists of family members.

Mildred R. Livingston. *Lanark, Perth and Richmond military settlements, Ontario.* Prescott: Livingston, 1987. 2 v. ISBN: 0-920992-23-4.
    v.1: census 1820-22; v.2: census-assessments, 1817-1822. Original records at the Archives of Ontario.

Glenn J Lockwood. *Smiths Falls, a social history of the men and women in a Rideau Canal community, 1794-1994.* Smiths Falls: Town of Smiths Falls/Heritage House Museum, 1994. 650pp. ISBN: 1-9692047-1-X. Index.
    Overwhelmingly large, but the index makes individuals accessible.

Duncan MacDonald. *The diary of deaths of Rev. John Macdonald (R.C.) c.1838 c. 1866.* Brockville: D.MacDonald, 1989. 246pp. ISBN: 0-921133-12-X.
    Transcriptions and translations (from the Gaelic) of notes made by a parish priest in Perth. Includes extensive family connections and details.

Duncan MacDonald. *Interesting notes & comments from the diary of Rev. John MacDonald, Catholic priest for 14 years (c. 1823-1837) at the town of Perth.* Brockville: Leeds & Grenville branch OGS, 1985-1988. 2 v. ISBN: 0-920-300-50-2 (v.1). Index.
    Volume 1 records visits the priest made to members of his flock in 1831 and 1834-5. Volume 2 (much larger) records gifts for the parish church in 1826. In both cases there are many personal observations about parishioners, of great value to genealogists.

Jean S. McGill. *A pioneer history of the county of Lanark.* Toronto: McGill, 1968. 262pp., illus. Bibliography.
    County history from a genealogist's point of view: many names.

J.R. Ernest Miller & Robert Sargeant. *Baptismal and marriage records of Presbyterian churches in Dalhousie and Lanark townships, Lanark county, Ontario.* Kingston: Kingston branch OGS, 1989. 91pp. ISBN: 1-55034-370-X.

J.R. Ernest Miller & Robert Sargeant. *1891 census returns for Ramsay twp., Lanark co., Ont.* Kingston: Kingston branch OGS, 1995. ii,70pp. ISBN: 0-7779-0510-8.

Alphabetical listing which also includes indication of residence of strays.

J.R. Ernest Miller. *Marriages, First Presbyterian Church, Perth, 1817-1857, by Rev. William Bell.* s.l.: s.n., 1987. 18pp.

Full listings for both bride and groom. Names, address, date and witnesses.

J.R. Ernest Miller. *Methodist church baptismal records, 1844-1875, Lanark county, Ontario.* Kingston: Kingston branch OGS, 1989. 50 leaves. ISBN: 1-55034-375-0.

These are from the Wesleyan registers. Computerized listing: name, address, parents, date of birth (date of baptism omitted).

J.R. Ernest Miller. *Presbyterian and Methodist church records of Pakenham, Lanark county, Ontario, 1830-1909.* Kingston: Kingston branch OGS, 1991. 49 leaves. ISBN: 1-55075-232-4.

Baptisms and marriages from Pakenham Methodist and St. Andrew's Presbyterian.

J.R. Ernest Miller. *St. Andrew's Presbyterian church, Perth, marriages 1830-1857; marriages 1858-1887; baptisms, 1830-1881.* Kingston: Kingston branch OGS, 1987. 32pp. ISBN: 1055034-022-0.

Robert Sargeant & J.R. Ernest Miller. *Baptisms, Perth Methodist circuit 1820-1842.* Kingston: Kingston branch OGS, 1986. various pagings. ISBN: 55034-043-3.

Name, birthplace, parents, birthdate.

Robert Sargeant & J.R. Ernest Miller. *Early settlers & Col. Marshall's 1834 report on conditions 1820-1822.* Kingston: Kingston branch OGS, 1987. 23pp. ISBN: 1-55034-035-2.

Includes a list of settlers dead before 1834.

Robert Sargeant & J.R. Ernest Miller. *1851 census returns, Lanark county, Ontario.* Kingston: Kingston branch OGS, 1989. 8 v.

Full text, families in alphabetical order. Pakenham not included; Ramsey missing.

Robert Sargeant & J.R. Ernest Miller. *1861 census returns, Lanark county, Ontario.* Kingston: Kingston branch OGS, 1993-94. 14 v. ISBN: 1-55075-258-8 (Bathurst)

Families listed alphabetically. The whole county is included.

Robert Sargeant & J.R. Ernest Miller. *Knox Presbyterian church, Perth, baptisms 1890-1924, Marriages 1858-1917.* Kingston: Kingston branch OGS, 1986. 33pp. ISBN: 1-55034-044-1.

Robert Sargeant & J.R. Ernest Miller. *Lanark county land transactions 1820-1847.* Kingston: Kingston branch OGS, 1991. 2 v. ISBN: 1-55034-925-2 (v.1)

v.1: 1820-1840; v.2, 1840-1847. Index includes buyer, seller, description, price, witnesses.

Robert Sargeant & J.R. Ernest Miller. *Some early Lanark county marriages not included in previous transcriptions of church registers.* Kingston: Kingston branch OGS, 1993. 103pp. ISBN: 1-55075-249-9. Indexes.

From a variety of sources at the Archives of Ontario. The cover says "1830-1869."

Robert Sargeant & J.R. Ernest Miller. *Some Perth area deaths from Perth Courier & Expositor records.* Kingston: Kingston branch OGS, 1987. 2 v. ISBN: 1-55034-042-5 (v.1)

v.1 covers 1919-1922; v.2, 1922-1929. Information in computerized chart.

Jean Steel. *Abstracts of births, deaths and marriages from the Almonte Gazette.* Privately published, 1994- . 8 v.

The years covered are 1867-1890. Available from the author.

James & Ann Wirtz. *Cemetery stone inscriptions, St. Bridget's cemetery, Stanleyville, N. Burgess township, Lanark Co., Ontario.* s.l.: s.n., 1981. 14,5pp., map. Indexed.

Leeds and Grenville Counties

Cemeteries for Leeds and Grenville are published by Leeds & Grenville branch OGS and Mildred Livingston.

Peter Andersen & Hubert Houle. *Mariages catholiques de la région de Perth...* SEE UNDER Lanark County

Births, deaths and marriages listed in the Kemptville Advance. Vernon: Osgoode Township Historical Society, 1988-   . (in progress) Index.
Extracts from the newspaper, full details not given. Various years are available from 1891 to 1917, including 1893-1905. The series is not published in chronological order, and the newspaper itself does not know if the missing years represent missing original copies.

D.J. Browne. *Census records for the township of Kitley.* Brockville: Leeds & Grenville branch OGS, 1992. 40pp. ISBN: 0-920300-86-3.
Various years from 1804 to 1844.

D.J. Browne. *Early census records for Yonge township, Leeds county, Ontario.* Brockville: Leeds & Grenville branch OGS, 1992. 3 v. ISBN: 0-920300-89-8 (v.1)
Each volume contains various years, extending from 1802 to 1848. Done in digest form, so several years' entries can be compared.

Census records for the four townships on the Rideau River. Brockville: Leeds & Grenville branch OGS, 1992. 2 v. ISBN: 0-920300-84-7 & 0-920300-85-5.
A digest of records for various years for Wolford, Montague, Marlborough and Oxford. One volume covers 1796-1817, the other 1813-1848.

Evelyn Purvis Earle. *Leeds the lovely.* Toronto: Ryerson Press, 1951. 174pp.
Separate, chatty chapters on social life, lakes, houses, villages, towns, people—and elopements.

1851 census of... Leeds county. Brockville: Leeds & Grenville branch OGS, 1990-91. 5 v. ISBN: 0-920300-74-X (Bastard)
    Townships are published separately, each volume with its own title. The five volumes are: Bastard, N.& S.Crosby, Rear of Leeds & Lansdowne, Kitley, Elizabethtown. Full families, but not all details are given.

1861 census of Kitley township. Brockville: Leeds & Grenville branch OGS, 1992. 81pp. ISBN: 0-920-300-82-0.
    Full transcription. The branch has also published the 1861 census of Yonge.

Families of Leeds and Grenville counties. Brockville: Leeds & Grenville branch OGS. 3 v. ISBN: 0-920300-40-5 (v.2)
    Brief essays on early families or individuals (not genealogies).

GCHS Reporter. Prescott: Grenville County Historical Society, 1989-1993. 4 v. ISBN: 0-921876-25-4 (Publication no. 92, 1993). Index.
    Three of the four volumes have the individual title *Births, marriages, deaths, Prescott papers* followed by the year. The fourth specifically extracts the *Telegraph*. Years covered are 1837 to 1914. The full text is given.

A.R. Hazelgrove. *Name and place index to Illustrated Historical Atlas of the counties of Leeds and Grenville, Ontario, by Mika Publishing, Belleville, 1973.* Kingston: Hazelgrove, 1975. 66pp.

Alice M. Hughes. *Index to the 1891 census of Ontario, Grenville county.* Ottawa: Ottawa branch OGS, 1991. 2 v.
    The two published volumes include Oxford, South Gower, Wolford, Kemptville, Merrickville.

Illustrated historical atlas of the counties of Leeds and Grenville, Canada West. Belleville: Mika, 1973. 103pp., illus. ISBN: 0919-302-69-6.
    Originally published by Putnam & Walling, Kingston, 1861-2. Includes maps with names. For an *Index* see Hazelgrove, above.

Lorna Johnston. ***Births, marriages, deaths notices from the Brockville papers, 1830-1849.*** Brockville: Leeds & Grenville branch OGS, 1989. 102pp. ISBN: 0-920300-66-9.
    Full text. There is also a second volume covering 1850-1869.

Thad. W.H. Leavitt. ***History of Leeds and Grenville, Ontario, from 1749 to 1879, with illustrations and biographical sketches.*** Brockville: Recorder Press, 1879. 200pp., ports.
    Includes some old cemetery stone inscriptions.

Edwin A. Livingston. ***Farmersville marriages (Athens), Yonge township, Leeds county, Ontario, 1858-1896.*** Prescott: Livingston, 1986. unpaged. Index.
    Full text, with brides' index. From a record at the Archives of Ontario, which (from the introduction) would seem to be a local registrar's copy. Farmersville became Athens in 1891.

Edwin A. Livingston. ***History of New Oswegatchie and the Blue Church Cemetery, 1780-1986.*** Prescott: Livingston, 1987. 147pp., illus. ISBN: 0-920992-03-X.
    An interesting volume which combines community history, a cemetery transcription and biographical/genealogical details on the locals. This is in Augusta township.

Edwin A. Livingston. ***Index, baptisms and marriages, Brockville and District, 1812-1848.*** Prescott: Livingston, 1985. unpaged. ISBN: 0-920992-19-6.
    Index to three papers printed by the Ontario Historical Society in their *Papers and Records*. The introduction gives full bibliographic details.

Edwin A. Livingston. ***Kemptville marriages, Grenville county, Ontario, 1858-1880.*** Prescott: Livingston, 1987. 26p. ISBN: 0-920992-24-2. Index.
    Full text. These marriages are all Anglican, from a source at the Archives of Ontario.

Edwin A. Livingston. ***Leeds & Grenville counties, marriage register, 1869-1873.*** Prescott: Livingston, 1991. 126pp. ISBN: 0-920992-37-4. Index.

Compiled from material at the Archives of Ontario, but before general availability of the civil registration ledgers. Full information is given.

Edwin A. Livingston. *Rev. Robert Blakey's baptisms, 1821-1841; banns, 1825-1854 and marriages, 1821-1827, parish of Augusta (Anglican).* Prescott: Livingston, 1988. 47pp. ISBN: 0-920992-28-5. Index.

Full text. Original records at the Diocese of Ontario Archives in Kingston.

Edwin A. Livingston. *Wesleyan Methodist baptisms 1843-1900, Leeds & Grenville counties, Ontario.* Kingston: Kingston branch OGS, 1990. 73pp. ISBN: 1-55034-914-7. Index.

Information given in the same format as the original registers.

Mildred R. Livingston. *The 1807 census of Elizabethtown township, Leeds county, Ontario.* Prescott: Livingston, n.d. 17 leaves. ISBN: 0-920992-06-4.

Names only, but includes full lists of family members.

Mildred R. Livingston. *1795, 1797, 1799 rateable inhabitants and 1820 census of Yonge township, Leeds county, Ontario.* Prescott: Livingston, 1981. unpaged. ISBN: 0-920992-12-9.

The tax lists have names only, but the census includes numbers of persons in the household, grouped by age.

2nd Regiment of Leeds militia, 1814. Prescott: Livingston, n.d. 8pp. ISBN: 0-920992-01-3.

Names and ages.

Douglas N.W. Smith. *By rail, road and water to Gananoque.* Ottawa: Trackside Canada, 1995. 120pp., illus. ISBN: 0-9697415-2-9. Bibliographical references.

Transportation history of Leeds and area, with a special emphasis on railways. Since many immigrants to inner Ontario passed here, it applies to many families.

Some early census, Augusta Twp., Grenville county, Ontario, 1796-1848. Brockville: Leeds & Grenville branch OGS, 1994. 119pp. ISBN: 0-920300-93-6.

A digest of early records. The computerized format simplifies comparing the various years.

Lennox & Addington County

Cemeteries for Lennox & Addington are published by Kingston branch OGS.

Barbara B. Aitken & Dawn Broughton. *Tracing your ancestors...* SEE UNDER Frontenac County.

Dawn Broughton. ***Lutheran church records, 1793-1832.*** Kingston: Kingston branch OGS, 1987. 61pp. Index.
Extracted from *Papers and Records* of the Ontario Historical Society, v. VI (1905). The records are from Lennox. More than one congregation seems to be represented; the original 1905 introduction is included, which is useful for those researching Lutherans in Lennox & Addington.

Census returns, 1851-2 of the township of Earnest town in the county of Addington. Kingston: Kingston branch OGS, n.d. unpaged.
Published by the branch for the Quinte branch, UEL Association, who prepared it as a typewritten copy exactly in the form of the original. Includes an *Index* by Cora Reid and Barbara B. Aitken.

Linda Corupe. ***Births, marriages and deaths from the Napanee Beaver, 1870-1896.*** Bolton. L. Corupe, 1993. unpaged.
Entries given in computer-chart format.

Linda Corupe. ***1861 census of Sheffield township, Lennox & Addington Co., Ont.*** Bolton: L.Corupe, 19--. 90pp. Indexed.

Linda Corupe. ***Index to the 1851 census of Lennox & Addington county.*** Bolton: Corupe, n.d 99pp. ISBN: 1-55034-021-2.
Alphabetical transcription.

Linda Corupe. ***Index to the 1861 census of Lennox and Addington Co., Ontario.*** Bolton: L. Corupe, 1993. 93pp.
Heads of families and strays.

Linda Corupe. ***Lennox & Addington county (Ontario) marriages.***
Bolton: L.Corupe, 1995-   (in progress). Indexed.
   Extracted from civil registration records. V.1 covers 1869-1880 (2142 marriages).

Linda Corupe. ***The Napanee letters of James McKitterick as printed in the Napanee Beaver & Standard, 1877 to 1885.*** Kingston: Kingston branch OGS, n.d. 291pp., illus. ISBN: 1-55075-231-6. Index.
   Letters, often humorous, mentioning individuals in Napanee.

Linda Corupe. ***1901 census of Richmond Twp., Lennox & Addington Co., Ont.*** Bolton: L.Corupe. 123pp. Indexed.

Linda Corupe. ***Wesleyan Methodist baptisms, 1834-1898, Lennox & Addington co., Ont.*** Kingston: Kingston branch OGS, 1990. 138pp. ISBN: 1-55034-913-9. Index.
   In chart form including full information. Followed by a second volume, *Wesleyan Methodist baptisms, 1834-1898, strays, errors & omissions* (1992, 1-55075-238-3).

R.W. Cumberland. ***The United Empire Loyalist settlements between Kingston and Adolphustown.*** Kingston: Jackson Press, 1923. 24pp.
   Bulletin no. 45 of the Departments of History and Political and Economic Science in Queen's University. A brief introduction.

Walter S. Herrington. ***History of the county of Lennox and Addington.*** Toronto: MacMillan, 1913. xii,427pp., illus. Indexed.

Walter S. Herrington & A.J. Wilson. ***The war work of the county of Lennox and Addington.*** Napanee: The Beaver Press, 1922. 278pp., illus.
   Although the local war work accounts lack names, the lists of soldiers are more detailed, and all those killed are given fine biographies. Some include places of origin in Europe.

Illustrated historical atlas... SEE UNDER Frontenac County

Lennox and Addington Historical Society. ***Papers and records.***
Napanee: The Society, 1909-   17 v.

Historical essays on various aspects of the county's history. A rich resource, neglected by genealogists.

A marriage register... SEE UNDER Prince Edward County

Janet Milligan & Catherine Wilson. *Historical bibliography of Amherst Island.* Kingston: Kingston branch OGS, 1983. 10pp.

Cora Reid & Barbara B. Aitken. *Census returns 1851-2 of the township of Earnest town in the county of Addington.* Kingston: Kingston branch OGS, n.d. unpaged. Index.
    Complete transcription with surname index.

Larry Turner. *Ernestown, rural spaces, urban places.* Toronto: Dundurn Press, 1993. 283pp., illus. ISBN: 1-550002-187-7. Index.

Larry Turner. *Voyage of a different kind* SEE UNDER Frontenac County

Russ Waller. *Adolphustown Loyalist families, including index to early census returns.* Kingston: R. Waller, 1989. 2d ed. 66,13pp., map. Index.
    Originally published 1988. "All known families descended from the 55 original Loyalists".

Russ Waller. *Adolphustown, Richmond & Sheffield townships, Lennox & Addington county, 1851 census.* Kingston: R. Waller, 1989. various pagings, map.
    Full transcription, with suggestions of other sources of information.

Russ Waller. *Amherst Island Loyalist links; a marital network file of the settlers & descendants of Amherst Island in Lennox & Addington county.* Kingston: R.Waller, 1987. 105pp. Index.

Russ Waller. *1851 census, Camden E. township, Addington county.* Kingston: Walrus Press, 1987. 145pp. Index.
    Full transcription, with index.

Russ Waller. *1851-52 census, Lennox & Addington county.* Kingston: R.Waller, 1994. 2 v.
    Full transcription with index. The two volumes now in print are Ernestown and Fredericksburgh.

Russ Waller. *1861 census, Fredericksburgh township, Lennox & Addington county.* Kingston: Waller, 1991. 83pp. Index.

Russ Waller. *1861 census, villages of Napanee, Newburgh, Bath, Lennox & Addington county.* Kingston: R. Waller, n.d. various pagings, maps. Index.
    Alphabetical listing of families. Includes "141 maiden names and 22 recently deceased persons." Waller's census transcriptions always include supplementary material from other sources, so may be worth examining even if you have already looked at the census itself.

Russ Waller. *1901 census, heads & strays index, Lennox & Addington county.* Kingston: R. Waller, 1993. 120pp.

Russ Waller. *Like rabbits in Ernestown! a marital network file of original settlers in 1784 of Frontenac, Lennox & Addington counties in eastern Ontario.* Kingston: R. Waller, 1986. Rev. ed. 211pp. Index.
    Genealogical listings connecting individuals and families from the Loyalist settlers in this area. Originally published 1985. Followed by a substantial *Supplement* (1987) and another volume, *Rabbits^3* (1987).

Russ Waller. *Rev. John Scott's Presbyterian birth register, Napanee & district, 1842-1916.* Kingston: R. Waller, 1987. unpaged.
    Hand-drawn recreation of the register. Scott's marriage register, 1853-1934, published in the same manner (1986).

Loral & Mildred Wanamaker. *Anglican registers 1787-1814, Rev. John Langhorn, Rector of Ernestown, Upper Canada.* Kingston: Kingston branch OGS, 1980. 105pp. Index.
    Ernestown became Bath. The parish covered most of the southern part of the county.

Lincoln County
Cemeteries for Lincoln are published by Niagara Peninsula branch OGS.

Denise Ayotte, Françoise Dubé, Yolande Laverdière. *Baptêmes, mariages et sépultures, paroisse Immaculée Conception, St-Catharines, 1924-1985.* Welland: Société franco-ontarienne d'Histoire et de Généalogie, Régionale du Niagara, n.d. 205 leaves.
"Paroisses de l'Ontario français, 9". Full information.

The capital years: Niagara-on-the-Lake, 1792-1796. Toronto: Dundurn Press, 1991. 256pp., illus. ISBN: 1-55002-149-4. Bibliography. Index.
A collection of essays, many of which would provide background for family histories concerning Loyalists or other early settlers in this area. Topics include military life, food, "at home in early Niagara township", inns, health and relations with the indigenous peoples.

Janet Carnochan. *Early churches in the Niagara peninsula...* SEE UNDER Welland County

Janet Carnochan. *History of Niagara.* Belleville: Mika, 1973. xiv,333pp., illus. ISBN: 0-919302-69-6. Indexed.
First published in Toronto in 1914. About the town of Niagara, now Niagara-on-the-Lake, first capital of Upper Canada.

Janet Carnochan. *Inscriptions and graves...* SEE UNDER Welland County

Census of Niagara, 1783. Hamilton: Hamilton branch, UEL Association of Canada, 1978. pp.198-214.
Original documents in the British Museum. Also published in the *Ontario Register.* Names and ages.

1828 census, Lincoln county. St. Catharines: Niagara Peninsula branch OGS, 1986. Rev. 30pp. ISBN: 0-920036-57-0. Index.
This census was heads of families only. This is a full transcription plus index. Clinton, Grantham, Louth and Grimsby are included. For Gainsborough, see their 1818 census index for Welland county.

Farmers' directory ca. 1891 for the county of Lincoln. Brantford: Brant County branch OGS, n.d. 2 v.
Photocopies from an old directory, one volume including Caistor, Clinton and Gainsborough, the other Grantham, Grimsby, Louth and Niagara.

Robert R. Halfyard. *Marriage register, 1884-1920, Grantham-Louth-Homer Methodist church circuit, Lincoln county.* St. Catharines: Niagara Peninsula branch OGS, 1993. 16pp. ISBN: 1-55116-838-3. Index.
Full text.

Illustrated historical atlas of the counties of Lincoln & Welland, Ont. Port Elgin: Cummings, 1971. 88pp., illus.
Originally published by Page, Toronto, 1876. Includes maps with names.

William Kirby. *Annals of Niagara.* Niagara Falls: Lundys Lane Historical Society, 1972. 269pp.
First published 1896. Important history, largely concerned with the peninsula up to the Mackenzie rebellion of 1837.

Lincoln Co. 1851 census. St. Catharines: Niagara Peninsula branch OGS, 1989-1990. 7 v. ISBN: 1-55034-331-9 (Caistor) Index.
Full transcription with index: Caistor, Clinton, Gainsborough, Grimsby, Louth, Niagara, Niagara township. There is no census for Grantham.

Lincoln county 1861 census. St. Catharines: Niagara Peninsula branch OGS, 1990-1991. 7 v. ISBN: 1-55075-002-X (Caistor) Index.
Full transcription plus index. Niagara town is not included.

Marriage register of Rev. Black... SEE UNDER Wellington County

Niagara Historical Society. *Publications.* Niagara-on-the-Lake: The Society. many volumes.
Pamphlets, first published in the late 19th century, including brief biographies, family histories, farm and house histories, more general topics.

The personal diaries of Andrew Thompson of Louth township, Lincoln county, Ontario, 1868-1890. St. Catharines: Niagara Peninsula branch OGS, 1989. 8pp. ISBN: 1-55034-327-0.

"An assemblage of vital statistics which pertain to various residents of Louth..."

Registers, 1884-1927, St. Ann's Presbyterian Church, Gainsborough Township, Lincoln county. St. Catharines: Niagara Peninsula branch OGS, 1994. 16pp. ISBN: 1-55116-835-9. Index.

Marriages only. Originals at the United Church Archives, Toronto.

Douglas A. Robbins. *1881 census, Gainsborough township, Lincoln county.* St. Catharines: D.Robbins, 1991. unpaged. ISBN: 1-895473-00-4. Index.

William J. Stevens. *Lincoln county industrial home.* St. Catharines: Niagara Peninsula branch OGS, 1989. 130pp. ISBN: 1-55034-329-7. Index.

This was the county poorhouse and old person's refuge. This excerpts all names appearing in the minutes 1883-1889.

Corlene Taylor & Gregory Miller. *1828 census, Lincoln county.* St. Catharines: Niagara Peninsula branch OGS, 1992. rev. ISBN: 0-9200036-57-0. Indexed.

Originally published 1985, revised 1986, revised again 1992. Complete transcription, with index.

Mary Kearns Trace. *Names in Lincoln county probates, 1794-1813.* Calgary, AB: Traces, 1986. 45pp. ISBN: 0921337078.

An every-name index.

Middlesex County

Cemeteries in Middlesex are published by London-Middlesex branch OGS.

Cl. T. Campbell. *Pioneer days in London; some account of men and things in London before it became a city.* London: Advertiser Job Printing, 1921. 128pp., illus.

Church of England (Anglican) subscribers in the county of Middlesex for the year 1864-65. London: London-Middlesex branch OGS, 1995. 33pp.

    1080 Middlesex residents, with the name of their parish church.

Evangelical pioneer, 1848-1850. Stratford: Bur-Mor, 1988. 9pp. ISBN: 1-55024-060-9. Indexed.

    Birth, death and marriage announcements from an early London newspaper, texts given in full.

Evangelical pioneer, May 13, 1848-April 11, 1850. London: London branch OGS, n.d. 8 leaves.

    This is an index only to the newspaper, referring to a card index with the complete information (not included) at the branch library. It is part of series of similar brief branch publications, which include *The Upper Canada Times, 5 March 1836* and *Western Globe October 23, 1845-May 10, 1851.*

The Heritage of Lobo, 1820-1990. Ilderton: Lobo Township Heritage Group, 1990. 456pp., illus. ISBN: 0-9694460-0-4. Index.

    Township history including family histories of those who lived here during the nineteenth century.

History of the county of Middlesex, Canada.... Toronto: Goodspeed, 1889. 1076pp.

    As well as general history, many biographies and family accounts.

Illustrated historical atlas of Middlesex county, Ontario. Belleville: Mika, 1972. 20,53pp., illus. ISBN: 0-919302-24-6.

    Originally published by Page, Toronto, 1878. Includes maps with names.

Index to names appearing in the London Free Press, 1 January 1849 to 1 July 1861. London: London branch OGS, n.d. 37pp.

    Over 7300 entries. This is an index only.

Fred Landon. *London and its vicinity, 1837-38.* Toronto, 1927. 31pp.
Material on the rebellion of 1837, with transcripts of original documents.

The London Advertiser. Stratford: Bur-Mor, 1988- (in progress) ISBN: 1-55024-056-0 (v.1) Index.
Extracts from the newspaper, chiefly births, deaths and marriages, given in full. Volumes 1-8 cover 1864-1869.

London and Middlesex Historical Society. *Transactions.* London: 1907-1967.
Historical essays and other materials. Since 1990, a new series of similar volumes has been published entitled the *London and Middlesex Historian.*

The London Free Press, 1 January 1849-1 July 1861, index of names. London: London branch, OGS, 1981. 37pp.
7300 entries, name and reference only.

The London papers. Stratford: Bur-Mor, 1987-88. 4 v. ISBN: 1-55024-045-5 (v.1) Indexed.
Collections of abstracts from short-lived newspapers or scattered issues, 1835-1893 (primarily 1836-1851). The principal papers are: *London gazette, Canada inquirer, London inquirer, London times, London herald, Western globe.* Mostly births, deaths and marriages, text given in full.

Hugh McColl. *Some sketches of the early highland pioneers of the county of Middlesex.* Ottawa: Canadian Heritage Publications, 1979. 58pp. ISBN: 0-920648-02-9. Index.
Originally published in Toronto in 1904. Long lists of names, with dates of arrival.

McGillivray township remembers, 1842-1992. Ailsa Craig: McGillivray Township History Group, 1992. 388pp., illus. ISBN: 1-55056-109-X. Index.

Donald E. Read. *An index of baptisms, marriages and deaths registered at Sacred Heart Roman Catholic Church, Parkhill, Ontario, and at St. Columba Roman Catholic Church, Bornish, West Williams*

Twp., Middlesex Co., Ontario, 1871-1990. Nepean: D.E. Read, 1990. unpaged. ISBN: 0-9690563-1-1.

Donald E. Read. *An index to the nominal census returns, West Williams Twp., Middlesex Co., Ontario, 1891.* Nepean: D.E. Read, 1986. 6,6pp. ISBN: 0-969056-3-8.
    Index only.

The Strathroy Daily Age, June-September 1878. Stratford: Bur-Mor, n.d. 7pp. ISBN: 1-55024-071-4. Index.
    Extracts, chiefly births, deaths and marriages, given in full.

Duren J.H. Ward. *Dorchester early settlers: living round-about the center of the township of North Dorchester, Middlesex county, Upper Canada from 1850 to 1870 as remembered by Duren J.H. Ward.* Denver, CO: Up the Divide Publishing Co., 1927. 96pp., ports.
    Virtual genealogies of some families.

Muskoka District

    Cemeteries *in Muskoka are not currently published by any group. SEE ALSO Note under Rainy River District.*

East Georgian Bay historical journal. **SEE UNDER** Parry Sound District

Gazetteer and directory of the county of Simcoe including the district of Muskoka... **SEE UNDER** Simcoe County

Guide book & atlas of Muskoka and Parry Sound districts 1879. Port Elgin: Ross Cumming, 1972. 112pp., illus.
    Originally published in Toronto in 1879.

Nipissing District

    Cemeteries *in Nipissing are published by Nipissing District branch OGS, and by the Upper Ottawa Valley Genealogical Group.*

Une bibliographie de sources historiques du district de Nipissing. North Bay: Société historique du Nipissing, 1979. 21pp.

Despite its publication under franco-ontarian auspices, most of the items in the bibliography are in English. Non-French-speakers should not be put off.

Julien Hamelin & Narcisse Courchesne. *Moyen-Nord Ontarien.* SEE UNDER Sudbury District

W.K.P. Kennedy. *North Bay past-present-prospective.* Privately published, 1961. 302pp.
Revised 1992. A history of the city, with many names. *Index* by C.F. Prong published separately by Nipissing District branch OGS in 1992 (ISBN: 1-55116-462-0).

Wilston Steer. *North words: highlights of the Near North's history.* North Bay: W.Steer, 1990. 240pp. ISBN: 0-9694577-0-77.
Brief historical essays on parts of Nipissing and Parry Sound districts.

Norfolk County

Cemeteries in Norfolk are published by Norfolk County branch OGS.

Assessments, township of Windham, 1809 & 1826. Simcoe?: Norfolk Historical Society, 1975. 29pp. Indexed.
Facsimile reprints plus typewritten interpretation.

Lewis Brown. *A history of Simcoe, 1829-1929.* Simcoe: Pearce Publishing, 1929. 108pp., illus.

Robert W. Calder & Dan Walker. *Wills in the Norfolk Land Registry Office, 1799-1900.* Delhi: NorSim Research, 1995. unpaged. ISBN: 1-896264-04-2.
Unprobated wills used to transfer inherited land directly through the registry office. These wills do not appear in the usual surrogate court records.

County of Norfolk directory, 1867; Norfolk county excerpts from the Oxford & Norfolk gazetteer and general and business directory first

published by Sutherland & Co., Woodstock in 1867. Simcoe: Norfolk Historical Society, 1984. unpaged.

John Earl. *A sketch of the county of Norfolk, Canada West.* Simcoe: Norfolk Historical Society, 1975. unpaged.
> Originally published in Simcoe in 1857. Essentially a directory.

Farmers' directory for the county of Norfolk. Brantford: Brant County branch OGS, 1983. 2 v.
> One volume contains Charlotteville, Townsend and Middleton; the other, Walsingham, Windham & Houghton. Dated 1891.

History of Delhi, 1812-1970. Simcoe: Second Ave. Printing, 1970? 204pp., illus.
> Includes biographies and family histories.

Irene Hopper. *Village of Delhi 1901 census.* Delhi: Norfolk County branch OGS, 1994. 17pp. ISBN: 1-55075-222-7. Index.
> Full transcription with index.

Irene Hopper. *Walsingham 1871 voters' list.* Delhi: Norfolk County branch OGS, 1994. 9pp. ISBN: 1-55075-224-3.
> Name, address and status.

Heather Ibbotson & Sandra Schuett. *Tracing your ancestors in Norfolk county.* Delhi: Norfolk County branch OGS, 1992. 28pp., maps. Bibliography.
> Brief handbook, useful summary of records.

Illustrated historical atlas of Norfolk county, Ontario. Belleville: Mika, 1972. 20,57,3pp., illus. ISBN: 0-919302-31-9.
> Originally published by Page, Toronto, 1877. Includes maps with names. For another edition of this atlas, see under Haldimand County.

Long Point settlers journal. Ridgeway: Log Cabin Publishing, 1994- quarterly.
> A small, intelligent journal to supplement *The Long Point settlers* and *Pioneer sketches of Long Point.*

Cheryl MacDonald. *Heritage highlights.* SEE UNDER Haldimand County

The men of Norfolk; produced for the 175th anniversary of the burning of Dover Mills, May 20-21, 1989. s.l.: s.n., 1989? 34pp., illus.
　　Includes names of early militia members.

Janice J. Miller. *1861 Norfolk county census index, Ontario, Canada.* Vernon, MI: J.J. Miller, 1984. 206pp., map.
　　Heads of families.

R. Robert Mutrie. *The Long Point settlers.* Ridgeway: Log Cabin Publishing, 1992. 274pp. Bibliographical references. Index.
　　Biographical references, each documented. "A guide for researchers in this area."

E.A. Owen. *Pioneer sketches of Long Point Settlement, or, Norfolk's foundation builders and their family genealogies.* Belleville: Mika, 1972. 572pp. Index.
　　Originally published in Toronto in 1898. Very important sourcebook for this area. Modern editions available. The index is inadequate, but a more complete *Index* by William R. Yeager was published by the Norfolk Historical Society in 1980.

Partial census of Woodhouse township, 1812. Simcoe?: Norfolk Historical Society, 1975. 32pp., facsim. Bibliographical references.
　　Issued as the first of the society's papers. Includes a facsimile of the original first sheet, plus useful comments.

St. James United Church, Simcoe, Ontario, marriage register, 1858-99. Delhi: Norfolk County branch OGS, 1990. 64pp. ISBN: 1-55075-205-7. Index.
　　This was a Wesleyan Methodist church at the time. Full text of the records, all names indexed.

St. Peter's Lutheran church, Rhineland, Norfolk county, baptisms, 1863-1902. Delhi: Norfolk County branch OGS, 1994. 57pp. ISBN: 1-55075-22-9. Index.

Name, dates of birth & baptism, parents. There is also a volume for this church of *Marriages 1858-1921; Deaths 1855-1916.*

Voters' list 1879, municipality of the township of Walsingham, county of Norfolk, Ontario, Canada. Lansing, Mich. : Mid-Michigan Genealogical Society, 1969. 22 leaves, map. Index.

Their Occasional papers, no. 2, with an introduction by Joanne Harvey.

Dan Walker. ***Our Lady of Lasalette parish register, 1856-1932.*** Delhi: Norfolk County branch OGS, 1990. 128pp. ISBN: 1-55075-054-2.

Full text.

Dan Walker. ***Records of St. Mary's parish, Simcoe, Ontario, 1858-1900.*** Delhi: NorSim Research & Publishing, 1994. 1 v. (various pagings). ISBN: 1-896264-00-X. Index.

This is a Roman Catholic parish. Listings include baptisms, marriages, burials, parish census of 1887 and relevant records from the cathedral in London.

Dan Walker & Robert W. Calder. ***Records of St. Peter's Lutheran church, Delhi, Ontario, 1854-1916.*** Delhi: NorSim Publishing, 1995. various pagings. ISBN: 1-896264-99-9. Indexes.

Translated from the German. Baptisms, burials, marriages, memberships, cemetery.

Dan Walker. ***Records of the south-west Norfolk pastoral charge of the United Church.*** Delhi: Norfolk County branch OGS, 1991. 59 leaves. Index.

Full text. Years covered: 1875-1904. Churches in Middleton, Courtland, Lynedoch.

Dan Walker. ***Records of the United Church, 1857-1900.*** Delhi: NorSim Research, 1994. 46 leaves. ISBN: 1-896264-02-6.

More accurately, records of several churches which are now United. Three are in Norfolk (at Delhi, Kelvin and Vittoria) and one in Oxford (Tillsonburg). Marriages and baptisms are included, but dates vary for each. Full transcriptions are given.

Dan Walker. *Records of Trinity Anglican church, Waterford, Ontario, 1849-1877.* Delhi: Norfolk County branch OGS, 1992. 11 leaves. Index.
Full text.

Dan Walker. *Saint Alban's Anglican Church register, Delhi, Ontario, 1850-1915.* Delhi: Norfolk County branch OGS, 1991. 62pp. ISBN: 1-55075-062-3. Index.
Burials, baptisms, marriages, with full text.

William Yeager. *Norfolk county marriage records, 1795-1870.* Simcoe: Norfolk Historical Society, 1979. 603 leaves. Index.
A massive undertaking, extracting marriages from many sources and collating their information.

William Yeager. *Norfolk co. marriages in the London district marriage registers, 1800-1855.* Simcoe: Norfolk Historical Society, 1987. 26pp.
Full text.

William Yeager. *St. John's Anglican church, Woodhouse, parish registers, 1830-1851, 1885-1948.* Simcoe: Norfolk Historical Society, 1982. 87pp. Index.
Full text.

William Yeager. *Searching for your ancestors in Norfolk county.* Simcoe: Norfolk Historical Society, 1982. 3d ed. 37pp. Bibliographical references.
Now outdated, this guide still deserves our attention because of the authority and reputation of the writer. He has only tentative plans for a new edition. SEE ALSO Ibbotson.

William Yeager. *Wesleyan Methodist Baptisms of Norfolk county, ca. 1842-1877.* Simcoe: Norfolk Historical Society, 1982. 61pp. Index.
Full text.

Northumberland County

Cemeteries for Northumberland are published by Kawartha branch and Quinte branch OGS, and by Susan Bergeron.

Susan Bergeron & Brian Tackaberry. *Brighton village census, 1861, Northumberland county, Ontario.* Brighton: S. Bergeron, 1992. 22 leaves. Index.
 Every name, but not all details. In the same series are Brighton village books for 1881, 1891 and 1901.

Susan Bergeron. *Census...* For other census transcripts by Susan Bergeron, see under Brian Tackaberry below.

Susan Bergeron. *Colborne village census, 1891, Cramahe township, Northumberland county, Ontario.* Brighton: S.Bergeron, 1993. 14 leaves.
 Every name, but not all details. In the same series are 1891 books for: *Seymour; Alnwick; Percy;* and *Campbellford*, all published in 1993 in the same format. See below under Tackaberry for *Brighton township; Cramahe; Murray.*

Susan Bergeron & Kate Gibson. *Haldimand township census, 1851, Northumberland county, Ontario.* Brighton: S.Bergeron, 1993. 53 leaves.
 Every name, but all details not given.

Susan Bergeron. *Haldimand township census 1891, Northumberland county, Ontario.* Brighton: S.Bergeron, 1993. 51 leaves. Index.
 Every name, but all details not given.

Allan N. Birney. *Oak Heights neighbours, 1800-1950.* Belleville: Mika, 1985. ix,271pp., map. ISBN: 0-919303-96-X. Indexed.
 Genealogies of families from this settlement, including parts of Cramahe, Haldimand and Percy.

Percy L. Climo. *Coburg Star, 1831-1849, births, marriages, deaths.* Peterborough: Kawartha branch OGS, 1985. 2 v. Indexed.
 Full text. Includes events far from Northumberland.

Linda Corupe. *Wesleyan Methodist baptismal register...* Bolton: L.Corupe. (in progress) Indexed.
   Brief volumes with extracts of Wesleyan baptisms from the registers at the United Church Archives. Townships already published: Brighton, Cramahe, Murray.

Edwin C. Guillet. *Coburg, 1798-1948.* Oshawa: Goodfellow Printing, 1948. 259pp., illus.
   Includes lists of politicians, soldiers. History in Guillet's usual anecdotal style.

Illustrated historical atlas... SEE UNDER Durham County

Ann Rowe. *Marriage register of Rev. Robert Neill, 1840-1878, Seymour township.* Bloomfield: Quinte branch OGS, n.d. unpaged. ISBN: 1-55114-731-0. Index.
   This church was Presbyterian. The same author and publisher have also published a volume of *Baptisms, 1852-1872* by this clergyman (ISBN: 1-55114-733-5).

Ann Rowe. *Marriage register of St. Andrew's Presbyterian church, Burnbrae, 1858-1886.* Foxboro: A.Rowe, 1986. 23pp.
   Full details. This church is in Seymour township.

Brian Tackaberry. *Brighton township census 1851-52, Northumberland county, Ontario.* Brighton: S.Bergeron, 1992. 41 leaves. Index.
   Every name, but not all details given. Susan Bergeron and Brian Tackaberry have produced other census books for Brighton township, all from the same publisher and in the same format: 1861 (1992); 1881 (1992); 1891 (1992).

Brian Tackaberry & Susan Bergeron. *Cramahe township 1851 census, Northumberland county, Ontario.* Brighton: S. Bergeron, 1993. 32 leaves. Index.
   Every name, but not all details are given. Material on known individuals added. The same publisher has published other census transcriptions for Cramahe: 1861 (1992); 1881 (1992); 1891 (1992), all by Susan Bergeron alone.

Brian Tackaberry. *Murray township census, 1851-52, Northumberland county, Ontario.* Brighton: S.Bergeron, 1990. various pagings. Indexes.

Every name, but not all details given. The same publisher and author have produced other census transcriptions for Murray: 1861 (1992); 1881 (1993); 1891 (1992), all in the same format.

Ontario County

Cemeteries in Ontario county are published by Whitby-Oshawa branch OGS.

Census of the village of Oshawa, 1878. Whitby: Whitby-Oshawa branch OGS, n.d. 41pp.

Names and addresses, no index. A typescript made in 1948.

J.E. Farewell. *Ontario County.* Belleville: Mika, 1973. 196pp. ISBN: 0-919302-66-1.

Originally published 1907. Includes "brief references to the pioneers and some Ontario county men."

Samuel Farmer. *On the shores of Scugog.* Port Perry: Port Perry Star, 1934. Rev., enl. 256pp., illus.

A history of Reach, including lists, biographical sketches.

Pat & Roger Harris. *Alphabetical index of the historical atlas of 1877 for Ontario county, townships of Whitby and East Whitby.* s.l.: s.n., n.d. 17pp.

Illustrated historical atlas of Ontario county, Ontario. Belleville: Mika, 1972. xii,63pp., illus. ISBN: 0-919302-23-8.

Originally published by Beers, Toronto, 1877. Includes maps with names. For *Index*, SEE UNDER Harris above.

Leo A. Johnson. *History of the county of Ontario 1615-1875.* Whitby: County of Ontario, 1973. 386pp. Bibliographical references. Index.

Gabrielle Lotimer. *Reflections of the past: the story of Rama township.* Washago: Township of Rama, 1989. 409pp., illus. ISBN: 0-9694088-0-3. Bibliography. Index.

The Oshawa Vindicator. Stratford: Bur-Mor, 1994- (in progress) ISBN: 1-55024-191-5 (v.1) Index.
    Extracts, chiefly births, deaths and marriages, given in full. Volumes 1-8 cover 1862-1871.

F.G. Weir. *Scugog and its environs.* Port Perry: Star Print, 1927. 143pp.
    A history of Scugog township (the island), formerly divided between Reach and Cartwright.

William R. Wood. *Past years in Pickering: sketches of the history of the community.* Toronto: William Briggs, 1911. 316pp., illus.
    Includes an alphabetical section of brief family histories, which may include dates of emigration and places of origin.

Oxford County

Cemeteries in Oxford are published by Oxford County branch OGS.

The axe and the wheel: a history of West Oxford township. s.l.: West Oxford Women's Institute, 1974. unpaged, illus.

Cathy Bechard & Eleanor Gardhouse. *Crown land register, Oxford county.* Woodstock: Oxford County branch OGS, n.d. unpaged.
    Name, description and date.

David Brearley. *Hotbed of treason: Norwich and the rebellion of 1837.* Norwich: Norwich and District Historical Society, 1988. 108pp., illus.
    A local account of the rebellion which was centred elsewhere. The author concentrates on individuals.

East Oxford Twp. deaths, 1872-1895. Woodstock: Oxford County branch OGS, n.d. 17pp.

Extracted from original township registrations in private hands. There is also a volume of births, 1872-1895 and marriages 1872-1895 (cover says 1883 only, but is incorrect).

Ruth Ellis, Margaret Phillips & Pat Newman. *Pre-registration marriages, 1854-1870 from Ingersoll Chronicle.* Woodstock: Oxford County branch OGS, 1991. unpaged.
Date, with bride's & groom's names only.

Mary Evans. *1891 Oxford county census index.* Woodstock: Oxford County branch OGS, 1989. 3 v.
Heads of families and strays index. Includes Blandford, Blenheim and Tillsonburg.

Guide to cemeteries & early churches in Oxford County. Woodstock: Oxford County branch OGS, 1991. 78pp.
A useful reference tool, summarizing churches, cemeteries, their locations and histories.

Ted Hoffman, Gerald Sharpe & Michelle Dew. *1891 census of Oxford county, township of Dereham.* Woodstock: Oxford County branch OGS, 1988. 115pp.
Full text, families in alphabetical order.

Illustrated historical atlas of Oxford county, Ontario. Belleville: Mika, 1972. xxiii,79pp., illus. ISBN: 0-919302-30-0.
Originally published by Walker & Miles, Toronto, 1876. Includes maps with names.

The Ingersoll Chronicle. Stratford: Bur-Mor, 1988- . (in progress) ISBN: 1-55024-063-3 (v.1). Indexed.
Part of Craig Burtch's series of excerpts from Victorian newspapers. The extracts are mostly births, deaths and marriages, given in full. Vols. 1-8 cover September 1854-April 1865.

W.A. MacKay. *Pioneer life in Zorra.* Toronto: William Briggs, 1899. 400pp., ports.
Personal reminiscence, replete with anecdotes of individuals.

Patricia Moody. *Mrs Canfield's people.* Woodstock: Oxford Historical Society, 1986. 84pp.
Extracts from a personal diary, including both BDM facts and descriptive material. Names in alphabetical order.

R. Cuthbertson Muir. *The early political and military history of Burford.* Quebec: Cie d'Imprimérie Commerciale, 1913. 371pp.
The military sections have the names of soldiers in the militia.

Ostrander Funeral Home, Tillsonburg, Index, 1910-1931. St. Thomas: Elgin County branch OGS, n.d. 18 leaves.
Name, date and cemetery; full information is available from the branch.

The Oxford papers: a composite. Stratford: Bur-Mor, 1989- . (in progress) ISBN: 1-55024-078-1 (v.2) Index.
Extracts from various newspapers from around the county, chiefly births, deaths and marriages, texts given in full. Volumes 1-4 cover 1840-1899.

The Oxford-Waterloo papers...
Despite the title, no Oxford newspapers are extracted in the single published volume of this series; however, many Oxford names appear in the *Ayr News*, which is included. SEE UNDER Waterloo County.

The Oxford Review. Stratford: Bur-Mor, 1991- . ISBN: 1-55-24-100-1. Indexed.
Similar to the series *The Ingersoll Chronicle.* Vol. 5 and following are entitled *The Woodstock review.* Vol. 1-5 cover August 1872- November 1875.

W.A. Ross. *History of Zorra & Embro; pioneer sketches of sixty years ago.* Embro: Embro Courier, 1909. 100pp., illus.

Thomas S. Shenston. *The Oxford gazetteer 1852.* Woodstock: Oxford County Council, 1968. 216pp., maps.
Originally published in Hamilton in 1852.

James Sinclair. *History of the town of Ingersoll*. Woodstock: Oxford Historical Society, n.d. 43pp.
>Written in the 1920s, covering the period up to the 1870s.

South of Sodom: a history of South Norwich. s.l.: South Norwich Historical Society, 1983. 414pp., illus.
>The 'index' in the front is actually a table of contents. There is an every-name *Index* published separately (1983).

James Sutherland. *County of Oxford gazetteer and general business directory, for 1862-3*. Ingersoll: Sutherland, 1862. 262pp.

The Tillsonburg Observer. Stratford: Bur-Mor, 1989- . (in progress) ISBN: 1-55024-079-X. Index.
>Extracts from the newspaper, mainly BDMs, text given in full. Volumes 1-2 cover 1863 to 1872.

Tillsonburg Public Library genealogy index. Tillsonburg: Tillsonburg Public Library, n.d. 7 v.
>Index only, of BDMs in the *Tillsonburg News*. Vols. 1-7 cover 1863 to 1935.

Township of Norwich 175 years. Norwich: 175th Anniversary Steering Committee, 1985. 184pp., illus. Bibliography.
>Largely a portrait of Norwich in 1985, with many pictures and names.

Dan Walker. *Beachville Roman Catholic mission, 1850-1853*. Delhi: Norfolk County branch OGS, 1992. 30pp. ISBN: 1-55075-210-3. Index.
>Covers a broad area: "Beachville, Woodstock, East Oxford, Windham, Norwich and Blenheim." Full text.

Dan Walker. *Records of Sacred Heart parish, Ingersoll, Ontario, 1850-1875.* Delhi: NorSim Research, 1994. 173pp. ISBN: 1-89626401-8. Index.
>Baptisms, burials and marriages, texts in full.

Dan Walker. *Records of the United Church...* SEE UNDER Norfolk County

Sam Weicker. *Church records of St. Matthew's Lutheran congregation, Plattsville, county of Oxford, Ontario, 1865-1904.* Kitchener: Waterloo-Wellington branch OGS, 1985. 12pp.

Extracted from the original records (now lost) and published in *Branch Notes* in 1976, then reproduced here.

Woodstock College memorial book. Toronto: Woodstock College Alumni Association, 1951. 165pp.

History of the college, lists of students, faculty, war records. This college was the origin of McMaster University in Hamilton, and had a Baptist affiliation.

Woodstock Social Register, Woodstock, Ontario, Canada, 1916. Woodstock: Oxford County branch OGS, n.d. 5pp.

Originally published by the Red Cross Club of the Hannah Lund Mission Circle, this lists women, their address and visiting day.

Woodstock Sentinel. Stratford: Bur-Mor, 1990-   (in progress) ISBN: 1-55024-095-1 (v.1). Index.

Extracts from the newspaper, mainly BDMs, with text given in full. Volumes 1-4 cover 1870 to 1874.

Parry Sound District

Cemeteries in Parry Sound District are not currently published by any group; however, an older transcription exists (see below). SEE ALSO Note under Rainy River District.

East Georgian Bay historical journal. Elmvale: East Georgian Bay Historical Foundation, 1981-   . (in progress) illus. ISSN: 0710-1279.

Historical essays by various authors; the volumes are produced irregularly.

Guide book & atlas of Muskoka and Parry Sound districts... SEE UNDER Muskoka District

Wilston Steer. *North words* SEE UNDER Nipissing District

These our ancestors were: records of those buried in public cemeteries, private family plots and any other burials located in the district of Parry Sound. Parry Sound: Senior Citizens Genealogical Society, Ontario Cemeteries, 1974/Bracebridge: Herald Gazette Press, 1976. 351pp. Index.

A substantial listing, but not to OGS standards. Finding individuals is difficult as the index is inadequate and the cemeteries are not identified by location, only by name. A better *Index* by a member of Nipissing branch OGS exists, but may be difficult to find.

Peel County

Cemeteries in Peel are published by Halton-Peel branch OGS.

Ruth M. Burkholder. *Peel county marriages in York county marriages registers, 1858-1869.* Stouffville: RMB Services, 1994. Revised. 35pp. ISBN: 0-921494-12-2. Index.

Originally published 1988.

Chinguacousy township collectors roll, 1855. s.l.: s.n., n.d. 12pp.
Name & address.

J. Brian Gilchrist. *Estate records of Peel county, Ontario, 1813-1867.* Toronto: Gilchrist, 1994. 42pp.

"An alphabetical index to wills, administrations and guardianships..." Limited circulation.

Halton-Peel marriages performed at St. Andrew's ... SEE UNDER Halton County

Murray Hesp. *Bolton school days.* Bolton: Bolton Enterprise, 1969. 147pp., illus.

An educational history of the village with many class pictures and names.

A history of Peel county, to mark its centenary as a separate county, 1867-1967. s.l.: County of Peel, 1967. 287pp., illus.

Illustrated historical atlas of the county of Peel, Ont. Port Elgin: Cummings, 1971. 72pp., illus.

Originally published by Walker & Miles, Toronto, 1877. Includes maps with names.

Mary Jones & Trudy Mann. *Halton-Peel marriages performed...* SEE UNDER Halton County

The Ruth Konrad Local History Collection: a selected bibliography of Canadiana. Mississauga: Mississauga Library System, 1995. 200pp.
An annotated bibliography of works on Mississauga and Peel county.

Jan Speers & Trudy Mann. *People of Peel; indexes to genealogical source materials.* Oakville: Halton-Peel branch OGS, 1981. 143pp.
Indexes to a variety of original sources.

Jan Speers & Ruth Holt. *Research in Halton and Peel.* SEE UNDER Halton County

Perth County

Cemeteries in Perth are published by *Perth County branch OGS.*

Assessment and population returns, 1836, 1842. s.l.: s.n., n.d. unpaged.
This is an early publication of Perth County branch OGS, giving census-assessment records for various townships.

The Atwood Bee. Stratford: Bur-Mor, 1992- several volumes (in progress). ISBN: 1-55024-148-6 (v.1.). Indexed.
Extracts from the local paper, mainly BDMs, given in full. Volumes 1-3 cover January 1890 to January 1894.

Eric Bender. *Magnified memories: the history of Wallace township.* s.l.: Wallace Historical Committee, 1990. 544pp., ill. ISBN: 0-9694132-1-1.
Includes lot-by-lot listings of occupants, and family histories.

Michael Bogues. *Perth county volunteer militia pay lists: 1868, 1869, 1870.* Stratford: Perth County branch OGS, 1986. unpaged.

Illustrated historical atlas of Perth county, Ontario. Belleville: Mika, 1972. xxv,66pp., illus. ISBN: 0-919302-22-X.
    Originally published by Belden, Toronto, 1879. Includes maps with names.

W. Stafford Johnston & Hugh J.M. Johnston. *History of Perth county to 1967.* Stratford: County of Perth, 1967. 478pp., illus. Indexed.

William Johnston. *History of the county of Perth from 1825 to 1902.* Stratford: Beacon, 1903. 565pp., illus.

William Johnston. *The pioneers of Blanshard, with an historical sketch of the township.* Toronto: Wm. Briggs, 1899. 278pp.
    Extensive biographies.

Malcolm MacBeth. *Mornington and its pioneers.* Milverton: Milverton Sun, 1933. 96pp.
    Mostly lists and biographical sketches.

Lynn Manktelow. *Mornington township 1879 name index, compiled from the 1879 historical atlas of Perth county.* Stratford: Perth County branch OGS, 1985. various pagings.

The Mitchell Advocate & county of Perth advertiser. Stratford: Bur-Mor, 1990-   . (in progress) ISBN: 1-55024-088-9 (v.1). Indexed.
    Extracts from the newspaper, mainly BDMs, given in full. Volumes 1-16 cover May 1860 to December 1878. Volumes 1-13 are entirely from the *Advocate*; beginning with v. 14 (1877), extracts from the *Mitchell recorder* are included. Some volumes may be exclusively from the *Recorder.*

Beryl Morningstar. *Perth county pioneers, 10th anniversary publication.* Stratford: Perth County branch OGS, 1993. 90pp., illus. ISBN: 1-55075-302-9.
    Essays on early families or individuals.

My roots are in Blanshard. s.l.: Blanshard Township, 1989. 220pp., illus.

Peterborough County

Cemeteries in Peterborough are published by Kawartha branch OGS.

William D. Amell. *Peterborough newspapers 1837-1856, Gazette 1845-1848; Despatch 1846-56; births, marriages, deaths.* Peterborough: Kawartha branch OGS, 1987. 136pp.

In addition to the extracts, there is a great deal more: passenger lists, histories of newspapers, maps, bibliographical advice.

Alan G. Brunger. *Harvey township, an illustrated history.* Buckhorn: Greater Harvey Historical Society, 1992. 483pp. ISBN: 0-9695677-0-7.

Jean Murray Cole. *The loon calls: a history of the township of Chandos.* s.l.: Township of Chandos, 1989. 138pp., illus. ISBN: 0-9694126-0-6. Bibliography.

Jean Murray Cole. *Origins: the history of Dummer township.* Warsaw: Dummer Township, 1993. 296pp., illus. ISBN: 0-9697481-0-8. Bibliographical references and index.

An outstanding example of the township history, not overwhelming but informative and crammed with names.

F. H. Dobbin. *Our old home town.* Toronto: Dent, 1943. 246pp.

A chatty portrait of early Peterborough.

A history of North Monaghan township, 1817-1989. s.l.: North Monaghan Historical Research Committee, 1990. 325pp., illus. ISBN: 0-9694335-0-6. Bibliography.

History of the county of Peterborough, Ontario; containing a history of the county; history of Haliburton county; their townships, towns, schools, churches, etc.... Toronto: Blackett Robinson, 1884. viii,783pp.

Illustrated historical atlas of Peterborough county, 1825-1875. Peterborough: Peterborough Historical Atlas Foundation, 1975. 127pp., illus.

This is the large format edition (45 cm.). An 'abridged version' (23 cm. and 279pp.; ISBN 0921880006) was also published.

Bill Labranche. *The Peter Robinson settlement of 1825: a story of the Irish immigration to the city and county of Peterborough, Ontario.* Peterborough: s.n., 1975. 80pp., illus.

Gayle Nelson & Joan Anderson. *Mather funeral home records, 1910-1922.* Peterborough: Kawartha branch OGS, n.d. 18pp. ISBN: 1-55075-480-7.
    This funeral home is in Peterborough.

Peterborough examiner, 1858-1875, births, marriages, deaths. Peterborough: Kawartha branch OGS, 1991. 203pp. Index.
    Full text.

Peterborough review, 1854-1868, births, marriages, deaths. Peterborough: Kawartha branch OGS, 1990. 212pp. Index.
    Full text.

Thomas W. Poole. *A sketch of the early settlement and subsequent progress of the town of Peterborough, and of each township in the county of Peterborough.* Peterborough: Peterborough Review, 1867. 220pp.
    At first glance, this seems to be about the town, but look at the subtitle again. Useful early sketches of the townships, including stories.

Prescott County

    Cemeteries of Prescott are published by Kingston branch OGS and Highland Heritage.

Julien Hamelin. *Répertoire des mariages, comté de Prescott, 1839-1974.* Ottawa: Centre de généalogie S.C., 1975. 561pp.
    Digest of marriages from 16 churches, all Roman Catholic.

Julien Hamelin. *Répertoire des mariages du comté de Prescott, 1863 à 1975.* Ottawa: Centre de généalogie S.C., 1978. 209pp.
    This volume was intended as the first of a series. These marriages are from four Roman Catholic churches in Hawkesbury. The volume above probably completed the series.

Illustrated historical atlas... SEE UNDER Dundas County

Nécrologie des pierres tombales, La Nativité, Cornwall. Ottawa: Société franco-ontarienne d'Histoire et de Généalogie, 1990. iii leaves, 75 pp. ISSN: 0823-1575 (Paroisses de l'Ontario français).
 Vol. 1 in the St-Laurent Region part of the series. This is a cemetery transcription.

Gabrielle Parisien-Bertrand, Louise Bertrand. *Baptêmes paroisse St-Jean-Baptiste, L'Orignal, Ontario, 1835-1992.* Ottawa: Société franco-ontarienne d'Histoire et de Généalogie, 1992. 2 v., illus. ISSN: 0823-1575 (Paroisses de l'Ontario français).
 Vol. 25 in the series. Name, parents, date.

Relevé des pierres tombales, Alfred, Ontario, 1871-1990. Ottawa: Société franco-ontarienne d'Histoire et de Généalogie, 1990. 76pp. ISSN: 0823-1575 (Paroisses de l'Ontario français).
 This is a cemetery transcription.

Sépultures, paroisse Nativité de la Bienheureuse Vierge-Marie, Cornwall, Ontario, 1887-1990. Ottawa: Société franco-ontarienne d'Histoire et de Généalogie, 1991. 209pp., illus. ISSN: 0823-1575 (Paroisses de l'Ontario français). Index.
 Vol. 22 in the series. Name, parents/spouse, date, age.

C. Thomas. *History of the counties of Argenteuil, Quebec and Prescott, Ontario.* Belleville: Mika, 1981. 694pp. ISBN: 0-919302-55-2. Indexed.
 Originally published 1896. Many family histories of early settlers.

Prince Edward County

 Cemeteries in Prince Edward county are published by Quinte branch OGS; many of their transcriptions are not available in book form but may be consulted in manuscript at their library.

Arthur Garratt Dorland. *Former days & Quaker ways, a Canadian retrospect.* Picton: Picton Gazette, 1965. ix, 198pp., illus.
 Second edition 1972, Mika. Autobiography of a leading Ontario Quaker. Full of atmosphere.

Elizabeth Hancocks. *1851 census of Prince Edward county, Ontario, Canada.* Agincourt: Generation Press, 1980. 179pp. ISBN: 0-920830-06-4. Indexed.
    Full census, in order, with surname index.

Angie Huizenga, Rob Stuart & Judy Scott. *Our Prince Edward county, a source reference.* Bloomfield: Prince Edward County Board of Education, 1982. 214pp. Index.
    A bibliography of both published and archival material.

Illustrated historical atlas... SEE UNDER Hastings County

Richard & Janet Lunn. *The county: the first hundred years in Loyalist Prince Edward.* Picton: Prince Edward County Council, 1967. 453pp., illus.
    Self-described as an "informal history", it is an outstanding example of the genre. Genealogists researching in Prince Edward are lucky to have it.

The marriage register, 1803-1823, of Stephen Conger JP Hallowell (from a copy at Ontario Archives) and Conger or White Chapel cemetery. Kingston: Kingston branch OGS, 1986. 12pp. ISBN: 0-920036-93-7.

A marriage register, 31 March 1836-3 Dec. 1838, Rev. John Hamm, Bay of Quinte. Kingston: Kingston branch OGS, n.d. 3 leaves.

Bob & Verona Milner. *Methodist church baptismal records, 1841-1888, Prince Edward county, Ontario.* Kingston: Kingston branch OGS, 1990. 91pp. ISBN: 1-55034-911-2.
    These are the Wesleyan records, with full text given.

7th Town Remembers. Ameliasburgh: 7th Town Historical Society, 1989. iv,220pp., illus. Indexed.
    Concerns Ameliasburgh township.

Patricia C. Taylor. *History of the churches of Prince Edward county.* Picton: Picton Gazette, 1971. 162pp., illus.

Potted histories of individual congregations. A useful reference tool for the second step in locating church records.

Rainy River District

There is little published material on many parts of northern Ontario. A canvas of public libraries in the principal towns indicates that, while they may have manuscript or archival resources for those who consult them directly, they have little to offer in the way of works that can be purchased. Use the **American Library Directory** *(listed in the general section of this book) to determine the address or telephone number of the public library in the town which interests you, and get in touch with them. The librarian will indicate what resources they have. Many local histories of northwestern Ontario are available from Singing Shields Productions, 104 Ray Boulevard, Thunder Bay P7B 4C4; write for a catalog.*

Renfrew County

Cemeteries *in Renfrew are available from Ottawa branch OGS, the Upper Ottawa Valley Genealogical Group, and Dolores Allen.*

Carol Bennett. ***Eganville, jewel of the Bonnechere, 1825-1991.*** Renfrew: Juniper Books, 1991. 238pp., illus. ISBN: 0-919137-23-7. Bibliography. Index.

Carol Bennett. ***Founding families of Admaston, Horton & Renfrew village.*** Renfrew: Juniper Books, 1992. 196pp. ISBN: 0-919137-26-1.
  Both genealogical and biographical information provided.

Carol Bennett. ***Founding families of Bagot, Blythfield & Brougham.*** Renfrew: Juniper Books, 1993. 156pp., map. ISBN: 0-919137-28-8. Index.
  Similar to Admaston volume, above.

Carol Bennett. ***Founding families of Grattan & Wilberforce.*** Renfrew: Juniper Books, 1992. 203pp. ISBN: 0-919137-27-X. Index.
  Similar to Admaston volume, above.

Carol Bennett. ***Wardens of Renfrew county.*** Renfrew: Juniper Books, 1989. 68pp., ports. ISBN: 0-919137-19-9. Index.
  Biographies and portraits of each.

Aldene & Les Church. ***Births, marriages & deaths: abstracts from the Renfrew Mercury.*** Renfrew: A.& L.Church, 1986-1991. 5 v. ISBN: 0-9692789-0-X (v.1) Indexes.

 Volumes 1-5 cover 1871 to 1921. Full text.

Norman Kenneth Crowder. ***Guide to the 1851 census of Canada West: Renfrew county.*** Nepean: Crowder Enterprises, 1987. 80pp. Bibliography.

 Heads of families and strays index.

Norman Kenneth Crowder. ***Renfrew county records, family history resources.*** Nepean: N.Crowder, 1990. 52pp. ISBN: 0-921536-00-3.

1851 census of Renfrew county, C.W. Ottawa: Ottawa branch OGS, 1989-1994. 2 v. Index.

 Full transcription plus indexes. v.1 (Horton) includes the 1842 census of Renfrew on folded sheets. v.2 contains Stafford & Pembroke.

Iris E. Elliott. ***Index to births, marriages & deaths in the Pembroke Observer and Upper Ottawa Advertiser, 1867-1898.*** Sault Ste. Marie: Sault Ste. Marie & District branch OGS, 1991. various pagings. ISBN: 1-44075-142-5.

 Information in computer chart format.

Genealogical extracts from the Eganville leader. Renfrew: Juniper Books, 1990-1991. 4 v. ISBN: 0-919137-21-0 (v.1)

 Volumes 1-4 cover 1902-1927.

Peter Hessel. ***McNab, the township.*** Arnprior: Kichesippi Books, 1988. 342pp., illus.

 Lists of soldiers, early settlers.

Louise Hope. ***Index to Horton-McNab Presbyterian baptismal and marriage registers, 1841-1883.*** Ottawa: Ottawa branch OGS, 1989. 51pp. ISBN: 1-55034-905-8. Bibliography. Index.

 Index only. Originals at the United Church Archives in Toronto. Useful introduction offering variant resources.

Illustrated historical atlas... SEE UNDER Lanark County

Madawaska Valley District High School Genealogy Club. *The 1881 census of Renfrew county.* Ottawa: Ottawa branch OGS, 1990 2 v. Index.

    One volume contains *Hagarty and Jones, Raglan and Radcliffe and Sherwood, Richards and Burns townships*; the other, *Algona South, Brudenell and Lynedoch.* Full text plus index.

Pembroke sesquicentennial 1978. Pembroke: s.n., 1978. unpaged, illus.

Alan Rayburn. *Geographical names of Renfrew county.* Ottawa: Geographical branch, Department of Energy, Mines and resources, 1967. 74pp., maps. Bibliographical references.

    Not a dictionary, but an essay, including references to persons.

Russell County

    Cemeteries in Russell are available from Ottawa branch OGS.

W. Allison Dempsey. *Growing up on the Castor river: stories of Osgoode and Russell townships in the early 1900s.* Vernon: Osgoode Township Historical Society, 1993. 69pp., illus. Index.

Hubert Houle. *Répertoire des mariages du comté de Russell, Ontario, 1858-1972.* Ottawa: Centre de généalogie S.C., 1978. 470pp.

    Digest of marriages from nine parishes.

Illustrated historical atlas... SEE UNDER Dundas County

Gabrielle Parisien-Bertrand & Louis Bertrand. *Baptêmes, paroisse St-Grégoire de Vankleek Hill (Ontario), 1855-1994.* Ottawa: Société franco-ontarienne d'Histoire et de Généalogie, 1994? 504pp., illus. ISSN: 0823-1575.

    Despite the title, the entries begin in 1878; earlier baptisms can be found in the records of L'Orignal and St-Eugène. This is number 27 in the series "Paroisses de l'Ontario français". See below for marriages and burials.

Gabrielle Parisien-Bertrand & Louis Bertrand. *Mariages, sépultures et annotations marginales, paroisse St-Grégoire de Vankleek Hill*

(Ontario), 1855-1994. Ottawa: Société franco-ontarienne d'Histoire et de Généalogie, 1994? 155,202,170pp. ISSN: 0823-1575.

For comments, see baptisms volume above. This is no. 27A in the series.

Simcoe County

Cemeteries in Simcoe are available from Simcoe County branch OGS, but three exceptions are listed below under Gianetto, Weber and Minesing.

Alliston funeral register, 1885-1908. Barrie: Simcoe County branch OGS, 1988. 53pp. ISBN: 1-55034-265-7. Index.

Records of Kinsey's funeral home, serving the townships of Adjala, Essa, Tecumseth and Tossorontio. Name, death date, age, place and price.

Josephine Boos. *The county of Simcoe, limited bibliography.* Barrie: J.Boos, 1988. 8 leaves.

Entirely concerned with historical/genealogical material.

Barbaranne Boyer & Michael A. Boyer. *Victoria Harbour, a mill-town legacy.* Erin: Boston Mills Press, 1989. 126pp., illus. ISBN: 0-919783-69-4. Index.

J. Herbert Cranston. *Huronia: cradle of Ontario's history.* Midland: Huronia Historic Sites and Tourist Association, 1951. 80pp., illus. Bibliography.

Background information for those with ancestry in the Establishments or northern Simcoe county.

East Georgian Bay historical journal. SEE UNDER Parry Sound District

Bernice Merrick Ellis. *Cemetery inscriptions, Tecumseth and West Gwillimbury townships, Simcoe county, Ontario, with historic notes.* Bond Head: Tecumseth and West Gwillimbury Historical Society, 1982. 339pp. ISBN: 0-9691367-0-6.

These transcriptions follow OGS standards.

Leslie M. Frost. *Fighting men.* Toronto: Clarke, Irwin, 1967. xxv,262pp., illus. Bibliography. Index.
    "The record...that one small town, Orillia, Ontario, played in the First World War." Includes list of soldiers with next of kin (not all from Orillia).

Gazetteer and directory of the county of Simcoe, including the district of Muskoka and the townships of Mono and Mulmur for 1872-73. Elmvale : East Georgian Bay Historical Foundation, 1985. vi,283pp. ISBN: 0-9691812-1-3.
    Originally published 1872.

Gazetteer and directory of the village of Orillia for 1866-7. Orillia: Orillia Historical Society, 1967. unpaged.
    Reprint of the original.

Stella M. Gianetto. *Midland's past inhabitants: tombstone inscriptions of the cemeteries of Midland, Simcoe county, Ontario.* Toronto: OGS, 1979. 214,65,22pp. Indexed.

Andrew F. Hunter. *A history of Simcoe county.* Barrie: Historical Committee of Simcoe County, 1948. 2 v., illus.
    Index by Elinor Sullivan published by SBI at Penetanguishene in 1992 (ISBN: 0-9696649-1-5).

Illustrated atlas of the county of Simcoe. Port Elgin: Cumming, 1970.
    Originally published by Belden, 1881. *Index* by Sally Walsh published by Simcoe County branch OGS in 1987 (ISBN: 1-55034-210-X).

Matchedash memories, 1888-1988. Coldwater: Matchedash Historical Committee, 1988. 153pp., illus.

Minesing Union Cemetery. s.l.: s.n., n.d. 28pp., illus.
    This tiny booklet has a summary of the burial records (names & dates). Published about 1965.

Mary Margaret Munnoch & Francis V. McDevitt. *Adjala.* Erin: Boston Mills Press, 1993. 256pp., illus. ISBN: 1-55046-104-4. Bibliography.

A general history of the township, with many personal references, and ninety pages of family histories at the end.

The Northern Advance. Stratford: Bur-Mor, 1991- . (in progress) ISBN: 1-55024-107-9 (v.1) Index.
Extracts from the newspaper, published in Barrie, chiefly births, deaths and marriages, texts given in full. Volumes 1-6 cover 1854 to 1871.

George R. Osborne. *Midland and her pioneers.* Belleville: Mika, 1975. 160pp., illus.
Originally published in 1939 as *A Story of Early Midland and her Pioneers*. Odd paragraphs written in the style of old newspapers, full of names and very interesting. An *Index* by Gwen Patterson was published by Huronia Museum in 1989.

Gwen Patterson & Bryan Gidley. *1860-61 population census for the townships of Tiny and Tay including the agricultural returns and the Reformatory.* Penetanguishene: Voyagers into Penetanguishene, 1992. 101pp. ISBN: 0-9693025-2-5. Index.
Complete transcription with index.

Penetanguishene 1875-1975. Penetanguishene: Town of Penetanguishene, 1975. 36pp., illus.

Pioneer history of Midhurst. Midhurst: Midhurst Historical Society, 1975. 2d ed. 122pp., illus.
Includes family histories.

Jack Purvis. *Index to probate & surrogate court records for Simcoe county, 1828-1929.* Barrie: Simcoe County branch OGS, 1988. 250pp. ISBN: 1-55034-267-3.
"Probates of wills, letters of administration, guardianships."

Rita Robitaille, Denis Maurice, Diane Fortin. *Mariages, Lafontaine (Ste-Croix) 1856-1982; Perkinsfield (St.-Patrick), 1909-1982; Penetanguishene (Ste-Anne), 1835-1982.* Ottawa: Société franco-ontarienne d'Histoire et de Généalogie, 1984. 224,53pp. ISSN: 0823-1575 (Paroisses de l'Ontario français) Index.

Names, date, place, parents. The churches are all Roman Catholic.

Elinor Sullivan. *A bibliography of Simcoe county, Ontario, 1790-1990.* Penetanguishene: SBI, 1992. 269pp. Index.
Includes a substantial section entitled 'Genealogy'.

Helen A. Wanless. *Simcoe county militia 1837; muster rolls and pay lists of the volunteers.* s.l.: Simcoe County branch OGS, 1990. 28pp. ISBN: 1-55034-281-9.

Eldon D. Weber. *Monumental transcriptions, volume 1: records of 60 burial grounds in central north Simcoe county.* Toronto: Ontario Genealogical Society, 1977. 163 leaves. ISBN: 0-920036-00-7. Index.
This was the only volume published in the series. The transcriptions are not to later OGS standards.

Stormont County

Cemeteries in Stormont are published by Highland Heritage.

Charles Fournier. *Répertoire des mariages de Cornwall, 1937-1979.* Ottawa: Centre de généalogie S.C., 1981. 402pp. Index.
Names, parents, date. Brides' index. This covers eight modern parishes.

Julian Hamelin. *Répertoire des mariages du comté de Stormont.* Ottawa: Centre de généalogie S.C., 1987. 276pp. Index.
Digest of material from five communities, all Roman Catholic churches.

John Graham Harkness. *Stormont, Dundas and Glengarry, a history, 1784-1945.* s.l.: s.n., 1972. 601pp., illus. Index.
Originally published 1946.

Illustrated historical atlas... SEE UNDER Dundas County

Mildred R. Livingston. *Pioneer Memorial cemetery...* SEE UNDER Dundas County

Duncan W. MacDonald. *Marriages, 1857-1896, St. John's Presbyterian Cornwall.* Brockville: D. MacDonald, 1988. 129pp. ISBN: 0-921133-15-4. Index.

    Originals at Upper Canada Village library. Full text. For earlier marriages, see below.

Duncan W. MacDonald. *St. Andrew's West (RC) parish register.* Brockville: Leeds & Grenville branch OGS, 1984. 5 v. ISBN: 0-920300-47-2 (v.1)

    Baptisms, marriages and burials, given in full, starting with 1804. Volume 5 continues up to 1891.

Duncan W. MacDonald. *The St. Columban's mission/parish, Cornwall, Ontario.* Brockville: D. MacDonald, 1991. 3 v. ISBN: 0-921133-46-4 (v.1). Index.

    The three volumes cover 1834 to 1890. Full texts of baptisms, marriages, burials, confirmations are given, and a great deal of other historical information.

Duncan W. MacDonald. *St. John's Presbyterian Church, Cornwall, births, marriages, deaths, 1833-1856.* Brockville: D. MacDonald, 1990. 189pp. ISBN: 0-921133-31-6. Index.

    Full text of entries. For later marriages, see above.

Edwin McDonald & Duncan W. MacDonald. *The story of St. Andrews West as recorded on the index cards of Edwin McDonald.* Brockville: D. MacDonald, 1987. 132pp. ISBN: 0-921133-03-0. Index.

    Miscellaneous notations about persons in St. Andrews West, with particular reference to the church and the original 38 families.

Clive Marin. Stormont, Dundas and Glengarry... SEE UNDER Dundas County

Sépultures, paroisse Notre-Dame-du-Rosaire, Crysler, Ontario, 1889-1977. Ottawa: Société franco-ontarienne d'Histoire et de Généalogie, 1991. 89pp., illus. ISSN: 0823-1575 (Paroisses de l'Ontario français).

    Vol. 23 in the series. Name, parents/spouse, dates of death and burial, age.

Sépultures, paroisse Saint-Columban, Cornwall, 1834-1977. Ottawa: Société franco-ontarienne d'Histoire et de Généalogie, 1989. 353pp. ISSN: 0823-1575 (Paroisses de l'Ontario français). Index.
    Vol. 19 in the series. Name, parents/spouse, dates of death and burial, age, witnesses.

James Smart. *Data on existing cemeteries...* SEE UNDER Dundas County

Marcel J.P. Yelle. *Répertoire de mariages de la paroisse de la Nativité de Cornwall, 1887-1969.* Ottawa: Centre de généalogie S.C., n.d. 519pp.
    Names, parents, date.

Marcel J.P. Yelle. *Répertoire des mariages de la paroisse Saint-Columban de Cornwall, 1829-1969.* Ottawa: Centre de généalogie S.C., n.d. 247pp.
    Names given alphabetically, with parents and date.

Sudbury District

Cemeteries in Sudbury are published by Sudbury & District branch OGS. SEE ALSO Note under Rainy River District.

William A. Campbell. *The French and Pickerel rivers: their history and their people.* Britt: W.A.Campbell, 1992. viii,328pp., illus.
    Includes family histories.

Narcisse Couchesne. *Mariages, paroisse Sainte-Anne de Sudbury, 1883-1983.* Sudbury: Société franco-ontarienne d'Histoire et de Généalogie, Régionale Sudbury-Laurentienne, 1983. 382pp. ISSN: 0823-1575 (Paroisse de l'Ontario français) Indexed.
    Volume 1 of the series. Names of participants, residence, parents and date only. This material, by the same author, was also published by the Centre de généalogie S.C. in Ottawa, possibly the same year, under the title *Répertoire des mariages, paroisse Sainte-Anne de Sudbury, 1883-1983.* The latter publication was intended as v.1 of the series *Moyen-Nord Ontarien* (q.v.), although not labelled as such.

Vincent Crichton. *Pioneering in northern Ontario: history of the Chapleau district.* Belleville: Mika, 1975. 407pp., illus.

Julien Hamelin & Narcisse Courchesne. *Moyen-Nord Ontarien.* Ottawa: Centre de généalogie S.C., 1984-1985. 10 v. Index.
    Marriage registers of Roman Catholic churches, similar to others from this publisher (names, parents, date, parish). The districts covered are Sudbury, Algoma and Nipissing, with the parishes stretching from Wawa and Dubreuilville in the West to Mattawa in the east, mostly in the vicinity of Highway 17. The first volume is meant to be that for St. Anne's, Sudbury (see under Courchesne, above) but it is not labelled as such; the series name begins with v.2 and runs to v.11.

Julien Hamelin. *Répertoire des mariages de Cochrane...* SEE UNDER Cochrane District (includes Chapleau, Foleyet, Gogama, Sultan)

Industrial communities of the Sudbury basin: Copper Cliff, Victoria Mines, Mond and Coniston. Sudbury: Sudbury Historical Society, 1986. 64pp., illus. Index.

Pioneer families, their odyssey, their settlement. Sudbury: Sudbury Public Library, 1980. 61,21 leaves, illus. Bibliographical references.
    Originally published in French in 1944 by the Société historique du Nouvel-Ontario. This translation by Ryan Taylor was meant to assist non-francophone genealogists. The book consists of tales of the earliest families in Sudbury, some in narrative form and some as genealogies. Added to the English version is a correction of the Côté genealogy as given, and the original newspaper article which is refuted by one of the essays.

Sudbury, rail town to regional capital. Toronto: Dundurn Press, 1993. 303pp., illus. ISBN: 1-55002-170-2. Index.

Thunder Bay District
SEE ALSO Note under Rainy River District.

Marie Fortier, Therese Daigle, Angela Wood. *St. Theresa's Roman Catholic church, Geraldton, marriage register, 1934-1951.* Geraldton: Geraldton Genealogical and Historical Society, 1985. unpaged.
    Names, parents, date. Also indicates if parents are dead at time of marriage.

Timiskaming District
Cemeteries in Timiskaming are available from the Temiskaming Genealogy Group and Nipissing District branch OGS. SEE ALSO Note under Rainy River District.

Doug Baldwin & John A. Dunn. *Cobalt: a pictorial history of the development of silver mining.* Cobalt: Highway Book Shop, 1978. 71pp., illus. ISBN: 0-88954-147-7.
    Interesting if your relation was a miner. On p. 42, there is a list of salaries.

Peter Fancy. *A guide to historic Haileybury.* New Liskeard: Temiskaming Abitibi Heritage Association, 1993. 40pp., illus.

Julien Hamelin. *Répertoire des mariages du diocèse de Timmins...* SEE UNDER Cochrane District

Illustrated guide to the history and heritage of Lake Temiskaming. New Liskeard: Temiskaming Abitibi Heritage Association, 1992. 25pp., illus.

Jean MacDougall. *That we may remember: telling of Cane, Barber and Tudhope townships, district of Timiskaming.* Cobalt: Highway Book Shop, 1976. 59pp. ISBN: 0-88954-084-5.

The New Liskeard Speaker index of births, deaths and marriages. New Liskeard: Temiskaming Abitibi Heritage Association, n.d. 3 v. Index.
    The period covered is 1906-1920. Full information in chronological order, with index.

Northern News, published in Kirkland Lake, births, deaths and marriages. Kirkland Lake: Temiskaming Genealogy Group, 1992- . (in progress) Index.

    Full information in computerized format, many abbreviations. Years not published consecutively. Ten volumes published so far, covering ten years in the period 1923-1937.

Bruce W. Taylor. *Index to the 1901 census, Temiskaming district.* New Liskeard: Temiskaming Genealogy Group, n.d. 25pp.

    Both alphabetical and by page.

The Temiskaming Herald index of births, deaths and marriages, 1905-1912. New Liskeard: Temiskaming Abitibi Heritage Association, 1993. various pagings. Index.

    This newspaper was published at New Liskeard. The listing of events is chronological.

Victoria County

    Cemeteries in Victoria are published by Kawartha branch OGS.

Canadian post, 1861-1867, 1874-1876; Victoria warder, 1870-1873, 1876-1882, births, marriages, deaths. Peterborough: Kawartha branch OGS, 1993. 218pp. Index.

    Full text.

Ross W. Irwin. *Family history index of the Canadian post, 1861-1920.* Guelph: R.Irwin, n.d. unpaged.

    The index is simple, to names and dates only. "All births, deaths and marriages are not listed, just those that contain more family history than a simple...notice." Useful feature: a list of newspapers servicing Victoria county.

Watson Kirkconnell. *County of Victoria, centennial history.* Lindsay: Victoria County Council, 1967. 2d ed. rev. & updated 324pp., illus. Indexed.

    First edition 1921.

Waterloo County

Cemeteries in Waterloo are published *by Waterloo-Wellington branch OGS.*

Rosemary Willard Ambrose. *Boyd Presbyterian Church, Crosshill, Ontario, communion roll and membership register, 1888-ca. 1937.* Kitchener: s.n., 1992. 6 leaves.
Extracts from church records now in private hands.

Rosemary Willard Ambrose. *Waterloo county churches: a research guide to churches established before 1900.* Kitchener: Waterloo-Wellington branch OGS, 1993. 278pp., illus. ISBN: 1-55116-966-5. Bibliography. Index.
Each church has a brief history, description and location of records and picture.

Elizabeth Bloomfield with Linda Foster & Jane Forgay. *Waterloo county to 1972: an annotated bibliography of regional history.* Waterloo: Waterloo Regional Heritage Foundation, 1993. xxx,739pp. ISBN: 0-9696936-0-5. Index.
The intensive indexing of this volume provides more than title access to the history of the county, including many names. A necessary tool for researchers in this area.

Elizabeth Bloomfield, Linda Foster, L.W. Laliberté. *The Waterloo township cadastre in 1861.* Guelph: University of Guelph department of geography, 1994. 105pp. ISBN: 0-88955-362-9. Bibliographical references.
Land records.

Elizabeth Bloomfield. *Waterloo township through two centuries.* Kitchener: Waterloo Historical Society, 1995. 480pp., illus. ISBN: 9699719-0-7. Bibliographical references & index.

A.E. Byerly. *The beginning of things...* SEE UNDER Wellington County

Ezra E. Eby. *A biographical history of early settlers and their descendants in Waterloo township.* Kitchener: Eldon D. Weber, 1971. 44,393,49pp. Index.

Eby's version published 1894-95 in two volumes. J.B. Snyder published a supplement in 1931. Weber's version republishes both, with an *Index* and supplemental material. Genealogies of the earliest Mennonite families in the area, mostly from oral sources.

A. Leone Hinds. ***Waterloo county marriages, births and burials, 1840-1849, as recorded in Wellington district by the clerk of the peace, Thomas Saunders.*** Kitchener: Waterloo-Wellington branch OGS, 1992. 30pp. Index.
From a civil record in private hands.

Frances Hoffman. ***Birth, baptismal and marriage registers for the Free Presbyterian congregation of Chalmers church, Winterbourne, Ontario.*** Kitchener: Waterloo-Wellington branch OGS, 1987. 86pp. Index.
Typewritten version of original holograph records, full text. Some of the records are not publicly available in any other format.

Illustrated atlas of the county of Waterloo (H. Parsell & Co., Toronto, Ont., 1881); county of Waterloo directory, 1877-1878 (Armstrong & Co., Toronto); Illustrated atlas of the county of Wellington (Walker & Miles, Toronto, 1877). Port Elgin: Cumming, 1972. 96pp., illus.
Includes maps with names.

Norma Huber. ***Marriages of Galt and area inhabitants with some strays.*** Kitchener: Waterloo-Wellington branch OGS, 1986. 34pp.
A digest of early Galt marriages (to 1869) from an assortment of resources. Full information.

David McKnight. ***Waterloo wills.*** Kitchener: Waterloo-Wellington branch OGS, 1993. 3 v. Index.
These are wills which were not probated, but are attached to documents in the land registry office. Full access to all names & indexes. Volume 3 is a maiden name index.

Kenneth McLaughlin. ***Waterloo, an illustrated history.*** s.l.: Windsor Publications, 1990. 208pp., illus. ISBN: 0-89781-416-9. Index.

Elizabeth Macnaughton & Pat Wagner. *Guide to historical resources in the regional municipality of Waterloo.* Waterloo: Wilfrid Laurier University Press, 1989. 118pp. ISBN: 0-88920-969-3. Index.

 A directory of places with archival materials.

Dona Madill. *St. Paul's United Church, Cambridge (Preston), Ontario, Methodist marriages,1897-1908, 1911-1912, 1923-1927, Preston circuit.* Kitchener: Waterloo-Wellington branch OGS, 1986. 18pp.

 Full text given. The branch has also published other records from this church by this author: *Methodist marriages 1909-1919, Preston Circuit; Methodist baptisms, 1907-1915, Preston Circuit* and *Methodist burials, 1908-1929, Preston circuit.*

Sue Mansell. *Marriages from the parish register of St. John the Evangelist, Church of England, Berlin, now Kitchener, Ontario, 1878-1889.* Kitchener: Waterloo-Wellington branch OGS, 1985. unpaged. Index.

 A hand-drawn reproduction of the register with full information. The branch has also published the same author's extractions of this church's *Confirmations 1870-1888* and *Burials, 1859-1890,* in addition to David Bowyer's *Baptisms, 1858-1872,* all in 1985.

Helen A. Moyer & Sheila Reinhart. *A journal of New Germany.* Maryhill: Historical Society of St. Boniface & Maryhill Community, 1991. unpaged, illus. Index.

 Chiefly extracts from the local newspapers concerning Maryhill (formerly New Germany), but with considerable added material about the church and school. Surname index for local families.

The Oxford-Waterloo papers. Stratford: Bur-Mor, 1989- (in progress) ISBN: 1-55024-083-8 (v.1) Index.

 Only one volume has been published so far, and it includes newspapers from Waterloo, Brant and Wellington counties, but not Oxford (Paris, Ayr, Guelph and Galt), covering the period 1852-1878. Many Oxford entries appear in the Ayr material. Extracts, chiefly births, deaths and marriages, texts given in full.

Barbara Stewart. *The Maple leaf journal: a settlement history of Wellesley township.* Wellesley: Township of Wellesley, 1983. 148pp., illus. Bibliographical references.

An *Index* by Paul Pepper was published by Waterloo-Wellington branch OGS in 1985.

Ryan Taylor. *Family research in Waterloo and Wellington counties.* Kitchener: Waterloo-Wellington branch OGS, 1986. 106pp., maps. Bibliographical references.

Although some of the information is somewhat outdated, the bibliographical references and other pointers to timeless resources are useful. The extensive church references have been superseded by Ambrose (q.v.).

Ryan Taylor. *Index to births, deaths and marriages published in the Hamburger Beobachter, 1855-1856.* Kitchener: Waterloo-Wellington branch OGS, 1985. 4pp.

Extracted BDMs from all surviving issues of this New Hamburg newspaper, translated into English.

Eldon D. Weber. *Assessment/collector's roll 1859, Waterloo township.* Kitchener: Waterloo-Wellington branch OGS, 1976. 16pp.

Name, location and occupation only.

Eldon D. Weber. *Waterloo county births as recorded in 1872 and 1873.* Kitchener: Waterloo-Wellington branch OGS, 1974. 15pp.

Full details as given in the original township registers. An *Index* by Marjorie Kohli was published with later printings.

Eldon D. Weber. *Waterloo county deaths as recorded in 1870, 1871, 1872.* Kitchener: Waterloo-Wellington branch OGS, 1973. 18pp. Index.

Early versions do not contain the index.

Samuel Weicker. *Church records of Strasburg Evangelical Lutheran Church, 1844-1893, Waterloo township, Ontario.* Kitchener: Waterloo-Wellington branch OGS, 1985. 7pp.

Baptisms, marriages, burials, confirmations and communicants, from original records now lost. Originally published in *Branch notes.*

Samuel Weicker. *Weddings, 1879-1912, Elmira Evangelical Congregation.* s.l.: s.n., 1991. unpaged.
  A manuscript listing, circulated in a very limited edition, with added pages describing original church records from several churches in the charge of the Trinity United Church, Elmira.

James M. Young. *Reminiscences of the early history of Galt and the settlement of Dumfries, in the province of Ontario.* Galt: Galt Public Library, 1967. ix,272pp., illus. Indexed.
  Originally published 1880 without the index. Young was the leading citizen of Galt in his time, and knew everyone, which his autobiography reflects.

Welland County

  Cemeteries in Welland are published by Niagara Peninsula branch OGS; some Niagara Falls cemeteries were published by Niagara Research (M Kamfoly-St.Angelo).

Denise Ayotte, Françoise Dubé, Yolande Laverdière. *Baptêmes, mariages et sépultures, paroisse St-Antoine de Padoue, Niagara Falls, 1955-1985.* Welland: Société franco-ontarienne d'Histoire et de Généalogie, régionale du Niagara, n.d. 70 leaves.
  "Paroisses de l'Ontario français, 8". Full information.

Baptisms register, St. Andrew's United Church, Niagara Falls, 1856-1892. St. Catharines: Niagara Peninsula branch OGS, 1993. 29pp. ISBN: 1-55116-840-5. Index.
  This church was Presbyterian at the time, in the town of Clifton (now part of Niagara Falls). The branch has also published this church's *Marriages, 1857-1878* (1994; ISBN: 1-55116-833-2). Full text is given in both.

Nicole Brochu, Denise Tassé, Christian Thompson. *Mariages et sépultures, paroisse Sacré-Coeur, Welland, 1920-1983.* Ottawa: Société franco-ontarienne d'Histoire et de Généalogie, 1985. 395-611pp. ISSN: 0823-1575.
  Vol. 7 in the series.

Nicole Brochu, Denise Tassé, Christian Thompson. *Naissances, baptêmes, mariages et sépultures, paroisse Saint-Jean-de-Brébeuf, Port Colborne, 1958-1983.* Ottawa: Société franco-ontarienne d'Histoire et de Généalogie, 1985. 90pp. ISSN: 0823-1575.
Vol. 5 in the series.

Nicole Brochu, Denise Tassé, Christian Thompson. *Naissances et baptêmes, paroisse Sacré-Coeur, Welland, 1920-1983.* Ottawa: Société franco-ontarienne d'Histoire et de Généalogie, 1985. 394pp. ISSN: 0823-1575. Vol. 6 in the series.

Donna M. Campbell. *All Saints Anglican Church, baptisms, register A, 1836-1886, Niagara Falls, Welland County.* St. Catharines: Niagara Peninsula branch OGS, 1993. 56pp. ISBN: 1-55116-844-8. Index.

Full details, in chronological order, surname index. The branch has also published the same author's transcriptions of *Baptisms, Register B, 1887-1901* (1993; ISBN 1-55116-846-4); *Marriage register 1840-1915* (1991; ISBN 1-55075-008-9); and *Burial register, 1848-1902* (1991; ISBN: 1-55075-016-X).

Donna M. Campbell. *Baptisms, marriages, burials, extracted from Register A (1820-1837), Holy Trinity Church, Portage Road, Niagara Falls, Ontario.* St. Catharines: Niagara Peninsula Branch OGS, 1992. various pagings, map. ISBN: 1-55075-005-4. Index.

Full details as given in the registers. The church is Anglican. The branch has also published the same author's extractions from *Register B, 1828-1927* (1992; ISBN: 1-55075-015-1) and *Register C, 1863-1947* (1992; ISBN: 1-55075-0019-4). All contain baptisms, marriages and burials.

Donna M. Campbell. *Cemetery transcriptions, burials & marriages, 1896-1916, Church of St. John the Evangelist, Stamford.* St. Catharines: Niagara Peninsula branch OGS, 1991. various pagings. Index.

This is an Anglican church, now within the city of Niagara Falls.

Janet Carnochan. *Early churches in the Niagara Peninsula, Stamford and Chippawa, with marriage records of Thomas and James Cummings, J.P. and extracts from the Cummings papers.* St. Catharines: Niagara Peninsula branch OGS, 1991. 100pp. ISBN: 1-55075-003-8. Index.

Originally published in the Ontario Historical Society papers for 1907. Republished here with an *Index*.

Janet Carnochan. *Inscriptions and graves in the Niagara Peninsula.* Niagara-on-the-Lake: Niagara Historical Society, n.d. 147pp., illus. Index.

"Reprint of no. 19 with additions and corrections." Very early reading of some stones in a variety of cemeteries in Lincoln and Welland, usually 'prominent' persons. Useful for checking in case the stones have been lost before later OGS readings.

James Cummings. *An intimate view of Welland county a century ago, from Robert Gourlay's "Statistical Account of Upper Canada."* Welland: The Tribune Telegraph Press, 1924. 23pp.

Observations of a traveller in the county in 1817.

1851 census. St. Catharines: Niagara Peninsula branch OGS, 1986-1992. Rev. 6 v. ISBN: 1-55075-011-9. Index.

A full transcription with index. Originally published 1985-6, revised 1992. There are separate volumes (with individual titles) for each township/village.

1861 census. St. Catharines: Niagara Peninsula branch OGS, 1986-1992. Rev. 13 v. ISBN: 0-920036-71-6 (Stamford) Index.

Full transcription, in order plus index.

Farmers' directory for the county of Welland. Brantford: Brant County branch OGS, 1983. 2 v.

Photocopy of sections from an 1891 directory. One volume includes Thorold, Wainfleet, Willoughby and Bertie; the other, Crowland, Humberstone, Pelham and Stamford.

From Esther Summers' collections: marriage records of Methodist church, Welland county, St. Catharines circuit. St. Catharines: Niagara Peninsula branch, OGS, 1990. 17pp. ISBN: 1-55034-337-8. Index.

Full entries dated 1858-1897 (very scattered).

Robert R. Halfyard & Harry Hood. *1828 census, Welland county.* St. Catharines: Niagara Peninsula branch OGS, 1992. Rev. 34pp. ISBN: 0-920036-58-9. Index.

Originally published 1985, revised 1986. The census was for heads of families only. This is a full transcription plus index. Gainsborough Twp. (Lincoln Co.) included here.

The history of the county of Welland, Ontario, its past and present. Belleville: Mika, 1972. 591,42pp. ISBN: 0-919302-16-5. Indexed.
First published in Welland in 1887, without the index. Stories from local history, including sketches of small settlements, names.

William Kirby. *Annals of Niagara.* SEE UNDER Lincoln County
Illustrated historical atlas... SEE UNDER Lincoln County

Carol M. Meyers. *Canada West census, 1851, Welland county, Ontario, vol. 1.* Saugus, Calif.: RAM Publishers, 1969. 107pp. Index.
Full transcription plus index. Includes township of Pelham and Chippawa only.

Pelham township, Welland county, 1836-1849 assessment rolls. St. Catharines: Niagara Peninsula branch OGS, 1985. 135pp. ISBN: 0-920036-60-0.
Name, address and amount.

Michael Power. *A history of the Roman Catholic Church in the Niagara Peninsula.* St. Catharines: Roman Catholic Diocese of St. Catharines, 1983. 226pp. ISBN: 0-9691586-0-2. Bibliography. Index.
Much of this has to do with explorers, but the later chapters might be helpful in locating family church record entries. The bibliography is extensive.

Records of marriage licenses issued at Thorold by Jacob Keefer, 1838-1874. St. Catharines: Niagara Peninsula branch OGS, 1991. 19pp. ISBN: 1-55075-018-6. Index.
Bride, groom & date only.

Registers of St. George's church, Drummondville, now Niagara Falls, Ontario; baptisms, 1836-1844; marriages, 1840-1844. St. Catharines: Niagara Peninsula branch OGS, 1985. 13pp. ISBN: 1-55034-324-6. Index.
Described as "a fragment from an old register". The Anglican church was a forerunner of All Saints, Niagara Falls.

Douglas A. Robbins. *Burial records and notations of William Dalton, 1845 to 1916.* St. Catharines: D. Robbins, 1991. 556pp. ISBN: 1-895473-07-1.

These records deal with Drummond Hill cemetery, and supplement the gravestone inscriptions published as *Historic Drummond Hill Cemetery* by Mabel Kamfoly-St. Angelo and Velma Rivard. Sometimes unusual details are included about the funeral or circumstances of burial.

Jennifer Lynn St. Angelo & Mabel St. Angelo. *1822 Stamford township assessment rolls.* St. Catharines: Niagara Peninsula branch OGS, 1992. Rev. 3pp.

Originally published 1983. Names only.

Corlene Taylor & Gregory Miller. *Wainfleet township, Welland county, 1849 assessment roll.* St. Catharines: Niagara Peninsula branch OGS, 1992. Rev. 11pp.

Originally published 1985, revised 1986. Name, location, amount of assessment.

Wellington County

Cemeteries in Wellington are published by Waterloo-Wellington branch OGS and by Kintracers.

A.E. Byerly. *The Beginning of things in Wellington and Waterloo counties, with particular reference to Guelph, Galt and Kitchener.* Guelph: Guelph Publishing, 1935. 106pp., illus.

Articles first published in the *Guelph Mercury*, folksy, factual and fascinating. Old-fashioned local history at its best.

Joyce Blyth. *Assessment roll for the township of Pilkington, 1858.* Kitchener: Waterloo-Wellington branch OGS, 1986. unpaged.

Full descriptive material, including age.

Marsha Boulton. *Families, facts & fables: Minto Memories.* Harriston: Township of Minto, 1988. 559pp., illus.

Lot-by-lot family histories. Usually known as *Minto Memories.*

Directory, county of Wellington, 1871-2. Fergus: County of Wellington, 1976. 238pp.
    Facsimile reprint of original 1871 edition.

Jack Dixon. *History of Maryborough township, 1851-1876.* Moorefield: Township of Maryborough, 1976. 101pp., illus.

A.D. Fordyce. *The monumental inscriptions in the cemetery at Belleside, Fergus, Ontario, Nichol township, Wellington county.* Kitchener: Waterloo-Wellington branch OGS, 1987. 32pp. Index.
    Originally published 1883. This represents the earliest stones in Belsyde, many of which may now be gone.

The Guelph Evening Mercury. Stratford: Bur-Mor, 1993- . 17 v. (in progress) ISBN: 1-55024-165-6 (v.1) Index.
    Another in the series from W.Craig Burtch, featuring full-text extractions from newspapers (mostly BDMs) with index. Volumes 1-17 cover 1864-1874.

Jean F. Hutchinson. *A history of West Garafraxa township.* Fergus: J. Hutchinson, 1989. 379pp., illus.
    Most of the book (pp.117-379) consists of family histories.

Illustrated historical atlas of Wellington county, Ontario. Belleville: Mika, 1972. 71,Lpp., illus. ISBN: 0-919302-27-0.
    Originally published by Historical Atlas Publishing, Toronto, 1906. Includes maps with names. For the 1879 atlas, see under Waterloo County.

C.J. McMillan. *Early history of the township of Erin.* Cheltenham: Boston Mills Press, 1974. 67pp., illus. ISBN: 0-919822-02-9.
    Originally published 1921. *Index* by Paul Pepper published in 1985 by Waterloo-Wellington branch OGS.

Marriage register of Elder Hugh Reid, Erin township, 1858-1875. Fergus: Wellington County Museum and Archives, n.d. 6 leaves.
    Marriages performed by a Baptist clergyman, including many from both Wellington and Halton counties.

Marriage register of Rev. Black, 1828-1842, districts of Gore & Niagara. Fergus: Wellington County Museum and Archvies, n.d. 7 leaves.
  Marriages performed by a Baptist clergyman, stationed first in Lincoln (Clinton-Louth), then in Wellington (Eramosa). Names of participants, residence and date.

Jacqueline McDonald Norris. ***Births, deaths & marriages extracted from Guelph advertiser, Jan. 1, 1847-Dec. 20, 1849.*** Kitchener: Waterloo-Wellington branch OGS, 1983. 24,viipp. Index.
  Full text.

The Oxford-Waterloo papers...
  Includes material from the Guelph *Mercury*. SEE UNDER Waterloo County

Ryan Taylor. *Early Anglican records: North Arthur.* Kitchener: Waterloo-Wellington branch OGS, 1986. 1 v.
  Volume 1: baptisms, burials and marriages, St. Paul's church, Mount Forest, Holy Trinity, North Arthur, 1858-1862. V.2 not published.

Ryan Taylor. ***Early church records of St. George's Anglican church, Harriston, including the Church of the Ascension, Clifford, baptisms and burials, 1858-1875.*** Kitchener: Waterloo-Wellington branch OGS, 1985. 9pp.
  Full information in computerized format.

Ryan Taylor. *Family research in Waterloo and Wellington counties.* SEE UNDER Waterloo County

Hugh Templin. ***Fergus, the story of a little town.*** Fergus: Fergus News-Record, 1933. 311pp.

Wentworth County

Cemeteries in Wentworth are published by Hamilton branch OGS.

Beverly Township crown patentees. Waterdown: Waterdown-East Flamborough Heritage Society, 1994. unpaged. ISBN: 0-921592-06-X.
    Useful introduction, but exact source of listings not indicated. Entries give name, location, size, registration date.

Mabel Burkholder. *The story of Hamilton.* Hamilton: Davis-Lisson, 1938. 183pp., illus.

Catalogue for Blachford & Wray burial records, 1851-1952. Hamilton: Hamilton branch OGS, n.d. 4 leaves.
    A Hamilton funeral home. See comments under Wallace funeral home catalog, below.

Catalogue for Dodsworth & Brown funeral home. Hamilton: Hamilton branch OGS, n.d. 7 leaves.
    Another Hamilton funeral home. These records cover 1897-1952. See comments under Wallace funeral home catalog, below.

Catalogue for Lorne G. Wallace funeral home, 151 Ottawa Street North, Hamilton, Ontario. Hamilton: Hamilton branch OGS, n.d. 4 leaves.
    This describes the records, but no names are given. Indexes exist and can be accessed through the branch or Hamilton Public Library.

John A. Cornell. *The pioneers of Beverly.* Galt: Highland Press, 1967. 366pp.
    Originally published 1889. Some general history of the township, but the personal sketches will be of interest to the genealogist. Farm histories. New edition updates village histories.

Crown patentees of East Flamborough Township. Waterdown: Waterdown-East Flamborough Heritage Society, 1992. unpaged. ISBN: 0-921592-02-7.
    Useful introduction, but exact source of listings not indicated. Entries give name, location, size, registration date.

Crown patentees, West Flamborough Township. Waterdown: Waterdown-East Flamborough Heritage Society, 1993. unpaged. ISBN: 0-921592-04-3.

Useful introduction, but exact source of listings not indicated. Entries give name, location, size and registration date.

Dictionary of Hamilton biography. Hamilton: Dictionary of Hamilton Biography, 1981- . (in progress) ISBN: 0-9691023-0-5 (v.1) Bibliographical references. Index.

Written in the format of the *Dictionary of Canadian biography.* Volumes 1-3 cover persons who died up to 1939.

Early marriage notices, East Flamborough Township, 1806-1859. Waterdown: Waterdown-East Flamborough Heritage Society, 1984. 21pp. ISBN: 0-9691858-1-2. Indexed.

From "a wide variety of sources". Material extracted for the publication concerned either residents of the township or those born there. 195 marriages, but the source is not identified. (There is a general listing of sources only.) Most entries in the format of newspaper marriage announcements of the time.

East Flamborough Township directory listing, 1865. Waterdown: Waterdown-East Flamborough Heritage Society, n.d. unpaged.

Township description and entries retyped from original Wentworth-Hamilton directory.

East Flamborough Township listing, 1875. Waterdown: Waterdown-East Flamborough Heritage Society, 1995. unpaged. ISBN: 0-921592-11-6.

Entries only, from the 1875 McAlpine Hamilton-Wentworth directory.

1851 agricultural census, East Flamborough Township. Waterdown: Waterdown-East Flamborough Heritage Society, 1985. unpaged. ISBN: 0-9691858-2-0. Indexed.

List of names from agricultural census, with address and size of farm. This is intended as a reference to lead researchers to the entry in the original only.

Farmers' directory for the county of Wentworth, ca. 1891. Brantford: Brant County branch OGS, n.d. 4 v.

Photocopy of parts of an 1891 directory. v.1 includes Ancaster and Barton, v.2 Beverly and Binbrook; v.3, the Flamboroughs; v.4, Glanford and Saltfleet. Hamilton was not included.

Flamborough marriage records, records from the former townships of Beverly and East and West Flamborough. Waterdown: Waterdown-East Flamborough Heritage Society, 1988-1991. 4 v. Indexed.
 Four volumes: 1794-1829 (ISBN: 0-9691858-5-5); 1830-1834 (ISBN: 0-9691858-6-3); 1834-1839 (ISBN: 0-9691858-8-X); 1840-1844 (ISBN: 0-9691858-9-8). From "a number of sources", which are given; however, the exact date of newspaper entries is not listed. Entries are transcriptions of original, so may include parents' names or other supplemental information. Every name index. If the wedding appears in more than one source, both are given.

Flamborough marriage slips: records from the former townships of Beverly and East and West Flamborough. Waterdown: Waterdown-East Flamborough Heritage Society, 1991-1994. 4 v. Indexed.
 Four volumes: 1869-1875 (ISBN: 0-921592-00-0); 1876-1880 (ISBN: 0-921592-01-9); 1881-1885 (ISBN: 0-921592-07-8); 1886-1890 (ISBN: 0-921592-09-4). Originals of records intended for civil registration authorities in Toronto; whether these were registered is not clear. The slips were preserved privately and are now once more in public hands. Information very full, including birthplaces, age, religion, parents' names (mother's maiden name sometimes).

Flamborough obituary notices, 1823-1859 ; records from the former townships of Beverly and East and West Flamborough. Waterdown: Waterdown-East Flamborough Heritage Society, 1989. 15pp. ISBN: 0-9691858-7-1. Indexed.
 From various newspapers, source given, exact transcription.

The Hamilton centennial, 1846-1946: one hundred years of progress. Hamilton: Davis-Lisson, 1946. 122pp., illus.

Brian Henley. *Hamilton our lives and times.* Hamilton: The Spectator, 1993. 115pp., illus. ISBN: 0-9697255-0-7.

Reprinted local history newspaper columns rich in information. There is also a sister volume, *The Grand Old Buildings of Hamilton* (1994).

Illustrated historical atlas of the county of Wentworth, Ont. Dundas: Dundas Valley School of Art, 1971. xviii,63pp., illus.
Originally published by Page & Smith, Toronto, 1875. Includes maps with names.

C.M. Johnston. *The head of the lake: a history of Wentworth county.* Hamilton: Wentworth County Council, 1967. 2d ed rev. 345pp., illus. Bibliographical references. Indexed.
A professional history, largely political.

Loyalist ancestors: some families of the Hamilton area. Toronto: Pro Familia Publishing, 1986. 318pp., illus. Indexed.
Introductory material on the Loyalists of the Niagara-Wentworth region, then family histories by members of the Hamilton branch, UEL Association.

Marriage records, West Flamborough township, 1817-1832. Waterdown: Waterdown-East Flamborough Heritage Society, 1987. unpaged. ISBN: 0-9691858-3-9. Index.
91 marriages, from a number of sources, which are listed. Full details.

Marriage register, Methodist New Connection Church, Waterdown, 1858-1876. Waterdown: Waterdown-East Flamborough Heritage Society, 1993. 13pp. ISBN: 0-921592-03-5. Indexed.
Extracted from original registers at the United Church Archives. 103 marriages, participants mostly from W.& E. Flamborough. Names of parents included.

Charles Pinch. *Anglicanism in Ancaster from 1790 to 1830.* SEE entry in General section

Township of West Flamboro, province of Ontario, 1850-1950, centennial celebration. s.l.: Centennial Committee, 1950. 217pp., illus.
Includes biographies and family notes.

Trades & Professions in East Flamborough Township, c1850-1860.
Waterdown: Waterdown-East Flamborough Heritage Society, 1983. 14 leaves. Indexed.
   Listings extracted from 1851, 1853 and 1857-8 directories.

Dorothy Turcotte. *Burlington, the growing years.* Burlington: Burlington Historical Society, 1992. 272pp., illus. ISBN: 0-9696575-0-1.

Sylvia A. Wray & Maurice H. Green. *Dundas Street, Waterdown, 1793-1993.* Waterdown: Waterdown-East Flamborough Heritage Society, c1994. 64pp., ill. ISBN: 0-921592-08-6.
   Heavily illustrated. A brief history of the main street of the village, including business histories and some family homes.

York County
Cemeteries in York are published by Toronto branch OGS.

Aurora marriages and deaths: an index to marriage and death notices in the Aurora Banner 1864-1969. Toronto: Toronto branch OGS, 1995. 290pp.
   More than 10,000 names, mostly from Aurora, King township and Whitchurch, cross-referenced to local and family histories.

David Boyle. *The township of Scarboro, 1796-1896.* Toronto: William Briggs, 1896. 302pp. Indexed.
   Lists of names and many individuals mentioned in the text.

Brown's Toronto city and Home district directory, 1846-47. Oakville: Halton Peel branch OGS, 1989. 77,124pp.
   Reprint of the original published by George Brown.

Ruth M. Burkholder. *Index to 1901 census for Whitchurch and Stouffville, York county, Ontario.* Stouffville: RMB Services, 1993. 30pp. ISBN: 0921494-08-4.
   Heads of households and strays index.

Ruth M. Burkholder. *Index to Whitchurch township residents as shown in directories and census, 1837-1891.* Stouffville: RMB Services, 1988. various pagings. ISBN: 0-921494-00-9.

A helpful digest containing an index to each census, 1861-1891 (for 1901, see above), plus directories, to aid in tracking 19th century residents of the township and Stouffville.

Ruth M. Burkholder. *Methodist baptisms in Whitchurch, 1843-1899.* Stouffville: RMB Services, 1994. 38pp.
Extracts from the general register of Wesleyan Methodist baptisms at the Archives of the United Church in Toronto.

Ruth M. Burkholder. *Peel county marriages in York county...* SEE UNDER Peel County

Ruth M. Burkholder. *Resources for genealogy in York region, Ontario.* Toronto: Toronto branch OGS, 1995. 2d ed. 30pp.
A brief guide, but containing many addresses.

The city of Toronto and the Home district commercial directory and register...1837. Toronto: Toronto branch OGS, 1987. 192, 45pp. ISBN: 1-55034-200-2.
Originally published 1837.

The Colonial Advocate, 1824-1833. Stratford: Bur-Mor, 1987. 65pp. ISBN: 1-55024-047-1. Index.
Extracts from the newspaper, chiefly births, deaths and marriages, texts given in full. The paper was first published in Queenston, then in Toronto, and includes notices from all over the province.

Commemorative biographical record of the county of York, Ontario. Toronto: Beers, 1907. 673pp.
Biographies of leading citizens and pioneers as determined by the editors of the time. An *Index* was published by Mildred Livingston in 1991 (ISBN: 0-920992-38-2).

Norman K. Crowder. *Inhabitants of Toronto, Ontario, 1846.* Toronto: Toronto branch OGS, 1993. 49pp. ISBN: 0-7779-00076-9. Bibliography.
Extracted from George Brown's directory of that year.

Norman K. Crowder. *Inhabitants of Toronto, Ontario, 1850.* Nepean: Crowder Enterprises, 1988. 56pp. ISBN: 0-9691766-8-6. Bibliography.
> Extracted from Rowsell's directory of that year.

Norman K. Crowder. *Inhabitants of York county, Ontario, 1850.* Nepean: Crowder Enterprises, 1988. 86pp. ISBN: 0-9691766-9-4.
> Extracted from Rowsell's directory of that year.

Directory of cemeteries in the municipality of Metropolitan Toronto and the Regional Municipality of York. Toronto: Toronto branch OGS, 1989. 101pp., illus., maps. ISBN: 1-55034-561-3. Index.
> There are 304 burial places listed, with locations, status, whether transcribed (now outdated) and advice. An essential tool for those working in York.

A.R. Hazelgrove. *Place and name index to Illustrated Historical Atlas of the county of York and of the township of West Gwillimbury and town of Bradford.* Kingston: Hazelgrove, 1977. 77pp.

Historical sketch of Markham township, 1793-1950. Markham: Historical Committee, 1950. 105pp.

History of Toronto and county of York, with the townships, towns, villages, churches, schools. Toronto: C.B. Robinson, 1885. 2 v., illus.
> Rather staid but (because of its size) comprehensive.

Jeanne Hopkins. *Jackson's Point, Ontario's first cottage country.* Erin: Boston Mills Press, 1993. 80pp., illus. ISBN: 1-55046-053-6. Index.
> A history of part of Georgina township.

Illustrated historical atlas of York county, Ontario. Belleville: Mika, 1972. xxii,75pp., illus. ISBN: 0-919302-35-1.
> Originally published by Miles, Toronto, 1878. Includes maps with names.

Victoria Kennedy. *A view of the Heights.* s.l.: s.n., 1992? 64pp., illus.
> An informal history of the Birchcliff Heights area of Scarborough. There are many of these brief histories of parts of Toronto and York county, now heavily populated but formerly rural or at least

having the character of a separate community. Begin searching for them at the local public library or the Baldwin Room, Metro Toronto Reference Library.

Shirley E. Lancaster. *Accessing burial records for large cemeteries in Metro Toronto and York region.* Toronto: Toronto branch OGS, 1993. 14pp. ISBN: 0-7779-0052-1.
    There are more than 300 burial sites in York; the largest are indeed large. This helps with finding your lost Toronto relations.

Jesse Edgar Middleton. *The municipality of Toronto, a history.* Toronto: Dominion Publishing, 1923. 2 v., illus.
    A surprising number of names for the history of such a large city, including lists of soldiers and a biographical section of leading citizens.

Christine Mosser. *York, Upper Canada, minutes of town meetings and lists of inhabitants, 1797-1823.* Toronto: Metropolitan Toronto Library Board, 1984. 185pp. Index.
    "The earliest record of the residents of the area that is now Metropolitan Toronto..."

C. Pelham Mulvany. *Toronto past and present, a handbook of the city.* Toronto: W.E. Caiger, 1884. 320pp. Index.

John Ross Robertson. *Landmarks of Toronto.* Belleville: Mika, 1976. 3 v., illus. ISBN: 0-919302-04-8 (v.1). Indexed.
    Originally published 1894-98. A classic, and available widely in its new edition. The text is crammed with detail and the drawings are very useful (and easily reproduced).

Charles Sauriol. *Pioneers of the Don.* Orillia: Hemlock Press, 1995. 340pp.
    Available from Toronto branch OGS. The Don river valley's history, including many family histories. The same author has published similar volumes: *Tales of the Don* (Natural Heritage/Natural History, 1984; ISBN 0920474306); *Trails of the Don* (Hemlock Press, 1992; ISBN 0929066103); *Remembering the Don* (Consolidated Amethyst Communist Communications, 1981; ISBN 0920474225).

Herb H. Sawdon. *The Woodbridge story.* s.l.: s.n., n.d. 177pp., illus.
 Internal evidence indicates a publication date in the mid-1950s. A great many names and business histories by street.

Henry Scadding. *Toronto: past and present, historical and descriptive, a memorial volume for the semi-centennial of 1884.* Toronto: Hunter, Rose, 1884. 330pp., illus.
 Business histories and biographies of 'prominent' citizens. More of the same in his general history *Toronto of old: collections and recollections* (1873).

Patricia Somerville & Catherine Macfarlane. *A history of Vaughan township churches.* Maple: Vaughan Township Historical Society, 1984. 440pp., illus. ISBN: 0-9692207-0-7. Index.
 Brief histories, but records are rarely mentioned.

Robert M. Stamp. *Early days in Richmond Hill; a history of the community to 1930.* Richmond Hill: Richmond Hill Public Library Board, 1991. 400pp., illus. ISBN: 0-9695376-0-3. Bibliographical references. Index.

Anne Storey. *The St. George's society of Toronto, a history and list of its members, 1834-1967.* Toronto: Generation Press for the St. George's Society of Toronto, 1987. 131pp.
 Members with dates of membership, plus officers, and burials paid for by the society. If an obituary or other source indicates a relative's membership in a fraternal society, check to see if they have published a list such as this one, or have an archives. A similar volume is Henry T. Smith's *History of St. Andrew's Lodge A.F. & A.M. no. 16, G.R.C.* (Toronto: Macoomb Press, 1922) which includes many names; masonic lodges often publish lists of members and histories of this kind.

Mary Kearns Trace. *Births, marriages & deaths, "The Globe", Toronto, Ontario.* Calgary: Traces, 1986- . (in progress) ISBN: 0-921337-00-0 (set)
 Volume one (1844-1847) is the only one published so far. Information in computer format.

The Upper Canada gazette. Stratford: Bur-Mor, 1991- . 2 v. (more to come) ISBN: 1-55024-104-4 (v.1) Indexes.

Extracts from the newspaper (published at Toronto), mostly BDMs, with full text given. Vols. 1-2 cover 1796-1828. Included in these extracts are bits from other newspapers: *The York gazette, The York weekly post, The York weekly gazette, The United Empire loyalist.*

Henry Wellisch. **Register of genealogical resources in Toronto.** Toronto: Jewish Genealogical Society of Canada. 1993. 99pp.

Prepared for the 12th summer seminar on Jewish genealogy in Toronto.

Whitchurch township. Erin: Boston Mills Press, 1993. 160pp., illus. ISBN: 1-55046-098-6. Bibliography. Index.

One last general title:

Post office householder directories. Ottawa: Canadian Post Office, 1964-1977. hundreds of volumes.

If you have lost a relation in the 1960s or 1970s, this title may help you to find them. For urban areas, you can use a city directory, but for rural residents, there is no equivalent. These postal directories will fill the gap. There is one for each federal riding not contained in a commercial directory, including rural routes of big cities. They list heads of households only. The drawback is that the first names must contain only four letters, so most people are listed by initials. Names given are shortened to four letters: Harold becomes 'Haro'. Occupations are also given in coded form.

Only one set of these volumes seems to exist in Canada. They are at the National Library in Ottawa. Other libraries may have scattered volumes for their area.

Publishers
All places are in Ontario unless otherwise stated.

Ontario Genealogical Society, 40 Orchard View Blvd., #102, Toronto M4R 1B9

OGS branches:

Brant County, Box 23030, Eaton Market Square, Brantford N3T 6K4
Bruce & Grey, Box 66, Owen Sound N4K 5P1
Elgin County, Box 20060, St. Thomas N5P 4H4
Essex County, Box 2, Station A, Windsor N9A 6J5
Haldimand County, Boc 38, Cayuga N0A 3E0
Halton-Peel, Box 70030, 2441 Lakeshore Road West, Oakville L6L 6M9
Hamilton, Box 904, LCD 1, Hamilton L8N 3P6
Huron County, Box 469, Goderich N7A 4C7
Kawartha, Box 162, Peterborough K9J 6Y8
Kent County, Box 964, Chatham N7M 5L3
Kingston, Box 1394, Kingston K7L 5C6
Lambton County, Box 2857, Sarnia N7T 7W1
Leeds & Grenville, Box 536, Brockville K6V 5V7
London-Middlesex, Grosvenor Lodge, 1017 Western Road, London N6G 1G5
Niagara Peninsula, Box 2224, Station B, St Catharines L2M 6P6
Nipissing & District, Box 93, North Bay P1B 8G8
Norfolk County, Box 145, Delhi N4B 2W9
Ottawa, Box 8346, Ottawa K1G 3H8
Oxford County, Box 1092, Woodstock N4S 8P6
Perth County, Box 9, Stratford N5A 6S8
Quinte, Box 35, Ameliasburg K0K 1A0
Sault Ste. Marie & District, Box 20007, 105 Churchill Road, Sault Ste. Marie P6A 6W3
Simcoe County, Box 892, Barrie L4M 4Y6
Sudbury District, Sudbury Public Library, Bag 5000, Station A, Sudbury P3A 5P3
Thunder Bay District, Box 373, Station F, Thunder Bay P7C 4V9
Toronto, Box 518, Station K, Toronto M4P 2G9
Waterloo-Wellington, Eastwood Square Box 43030, Kitchener N2H 6S9
Whitby-Oshawa, Box 174, Whitby L1N 5S1

Albemarle Township Historical Society, RR #6, Wiarton N0H 2T0
Dolores Allen, 1156 Maybank St., Ottawa K2C 2W6
Allen County Public Library Foundation, Box 2270, Fort Wayne IN USA 46801-2270.
Susan Bergeron, 102 Prince Edward Street, Box 782, Brighton K0K 1H0
Lois Black, 196 Glengarry Avenue, Toronto M5M 1E2
Boston Mills Press, 132 Main Street, Erin N0B 1T0
British Isles Family History Society of Ottawa, Box 38026, Ottawa K2C 1N0
Bruce County Genealogical Society, Box 1083, Port Elgin N0H 2C0
Bur-Mor, 359 West Gore, Stratford N5A 1K9
Burlington Historical Society, 3062 Woodward Avenue, Burlington L7N 2M2
Canadian Council of Archivists, 344 Wellington Street, Room 1009, Ottawa K1A 0N3
Canadian Institute for Historical Microreproduction (CIHM), 395 Wellington Street, Ottawa K1A 0N4
Centre de Généalogie S.C., 240 Daly Avenue, Ottawa K1N 6G2
Aldene & Les Church, 15 Lorne Street North, Renfrew K7V 1K8
Linda Corupe, 210 Allan Drive, Bolton L7E 1Y7
Melba Croft, 1-114-7th Street East, Owen Sound N4K 1H7
Crowder Enterprises, 22 Canter Boulevard, Nepean K2G 2M2
Grant Curtis, RR #1, Lindsay K9V 4R1
Dufferin County Museum and Archives, Box 120, Rosemont L0N 1R0
East Durham Historical Society, Box 116, Port Hope L1A 3V9
East Georgian Bay Historical Foundation, Box 518, Elmvale L0L 1P0
Esquesing Historical Society, Box 51, Georgetown L7G 4T1
Genealogical Publishing, 1001 N. Calvert Street, Baltimore MD USA 21202
Genealogical Research Library, 100 Adelaide St. West, 5th floor, Toronto M5H 1S3
Generation Press, 172 King Henrys Boulevard, Agincourt M1T 2V6
Geraldton Genealogical and Historical Society, Geraldton P0T 1M0
Halfyard Heritage, 9 Frontenac Drive, St. Catharines L2M 2E1
Haliburton Highlands Genealogical Group, Box 567, Minden K0M 2K0
Hamilton Spectator, 44 Frid Street, Hamilton L8N 3G3
Heritage Books, 1540 Pointer Ridge Place, Suite 301, Bowie MD USA 20716

Heritage House Museum, Old Slys Road, Box 695, Smiths Falls K7A 4T6
Heronwood Writing Services, RR #2, Nanticoke N0A 1L0
Highland Heritage, RR #1, Lancaster K0C 1N0
Highway Book Shop, Cobalt P0J 1C0
Historical Society of St. Boniface & Maryhill Community, Box 123, Maryhill N0B 2B0
Hunterdon House, 38 Swan Street, Lambertville NJ 08530 USA
Huronia Museum, Box 638, Midland L4R 4P4
Juniper Books, RR #2, Renfrew K7V 3Z5
A. Gordon Keys, RR #3, Ayr N0B 1E0
Kichesippi Books, Stewart Lane, Waba, RR #2, Arnprior K7S 3G9
Kintracers, Box 48271, Midlake RPO, Calgary AB T2X 3C7
Lanark County Genealogical Society, c/o Marion Cavanagh, RR #1, Pakenham K0A 2X0
Mildred Livingston, St. Lawrence Court, RR #1, Prescott K0E 1T0
Log Cabin Publishing, 244 Maple Leaf Avenue North, RR#2, Ridgeway L0S 1N0
Duncan MacDonald, 268 Bartholomew Street, Brockville K6V 2S6
Donald McKenzie, 32 Morris Street, Ottawa K1S 4A7
Mississauga Library System, 301 Burnhamthorpe Road West, Mississauga L5B 3Y3
Multicultural History Society of Ontario, 43 Queen's Park Crescent East, Toronto M5S 2C3
National Library of Canada, 395 Wellington Street, Ottawa K1A 0N4
Natural Heritage/Natural History, Box 95, Station O, Toronto M4A 2M8
Niagara Research, Box 338, St. Davids L0S 1P0
Norfolk Historical Society, 109 Norfolk Street South, Simcoe N3Y 2W3
NorSim Research and Publishing, 157 Ann Street, Delhi N4B 1H8
Nor-West Genealogical and Historical Society, Box 124, Vermilion Bay P0V 2V0
Ontario Indexing Services, 351 Pommel Gate Cres., Waterloo N2L 5X7
Ontario Library Association, 303 - 100 Lombard St., Toronto M5C 1M3
Osgoode Township Historical Society, Box 74, Vernon K0A 3J0
Past to Present, 700 St. Clair Parkway, Corunna N0N 1G0
Pro Familia Publishing, 128 Gilmour Avenue, Toronto M6P 3B3
Diane Snyder Ptak, 12 Tice Road, Albany NY USA 12203
Quintin Publications, 28 Felsmere Ave. Pawtucket RI 02861-2903 USA
RMB Services, 251 Second Street, Stouffville L4A 1B9

Donald E. Read, 1181 Deer Park Road, Nepean K2E 6H4
Joy Reisinger, 1020 Central Avenue, Sparta WI USA 54656
Round Tower Books, Box 12407, Fort Wayne IN USA 46863-2407
SBI, Box 1081, Penetanguishene L0K 1P0
7th Town Historical Society, Box 35, Ameliasburgh K0K 1A0
Shenrone Enterprises, 38 Springhome Road, Barrie L4N 2W8
Société franco-ontarienne d'Histoire et de Généalogie, C.P. 720, Succ. B, Ottawa K1P 5P8
Jean Steel, RR #3, Almonte K0A 1A0
Wilston Steer, RR #1 Callander P0H 1H0
Sudbury Public Library, 74 Mackenzie Street, Sudbury P3C 4X8
Corlene Taylor, RR #1, Beamsville L0R 1B0
Temiskaming Abitibi Heritage Association, c/o Bruce Taylor, Box 1568, New Liskeard P0J 1P0
Temiskaming Genealogy Group, c/o C. Blackburn, 25 Algonquin Avenue, Kirkland Lake P2N 1C1
Tillsonburg Public Library, 2 Library Lane, Tillsonburg N4G 4S7
Traces, 1024 Motherwell Road NE, Calgary AB T2E 6E7
University Microfilms International, 300 N. Zeeb Road, Ann Arbor MI USA 48106
Upper Canada Village Reference Library, Upper Canada Village, RR #1, Morrisburg K0C 1X0.
Upper Ottawa Valley Genealogical Group, Box 972, Pembroke K8A 7M5
Vaughan Township Historical Society, Box 51, Maple L0J 1E0
Voyagers in Penetanguishene, Box 723, Penetanguishene L0K 1P0
Russ Waller, 114 Robert Wallace Drive, Kingston K7M 1Y2
Waterdown-East Flamborough Heritage Society, Box 1044, Waterdown L0R 2H0
Waterloo Historical Society, c/o Kitchener Public Library, 85 Queen Street North, Kitchener N2H 2H1
Waterloo Regional Heritage Foundation, c/o Susan Hoffman, Kitchener Public Library, 85 Queen St. N., Kitchener N2H 2H1
Westgarth, 46 Burnhill Bay, Winnipeg MB R3T 5N3
Wordforce, c/o Wendy Cameron, 305 Heath Street East, Toronto M4T 1T3
Young & Hogan Publishing, 331 Bland (14th Line), RR #2, Cavan L0A 1C0
Distributor of books and supplies: Global Genealogical Supply, 158 Laurier Avenue, Milton L9T 4S2